S TUDIO **P** APERBACK

HANS FREI

Louis Henry Sullivan

Zürich · München · London

© 1992 Artemis Verlags-AG, Zürich

Übersetzung ins Englische / English translation:
Sandra Brandeberry
Gestaltung / Design: Urs Berger-Pecora

Printed in Germany
ISBN 3-7608-8131-9
ISBN 1-874056-15-3

Inhalt

Contents

Vorwort

Preface

Nur ein kleiner Teil der Bauten, die Louis Sullivan allein oder zusammen mit seinem Partner Dankmar Adler errichtet hat, hielt dem ökonomischen Druck stand und ist uns erhalten geblieben. Viele sind jedoch hervorragend dokumentiert. Zum einen dank Henry Fuermann, der Sullivans Bauten zusammen mit seinen Söhnen Leon und Clarence jeweils kurz nach Fertigstellung photographierte (die Aufnahmen stammen wahrscheinlich vor allem von Clarence). Zum andern dank Richard Nickel, der die Zerstörung der Bauten immer wieder zu verhindern suchte. Er kam tragischerweise im Bauschutt des Chicago Stock Exchange Building von Adler & Sullivan ums Leben.

Einigen Personen habe ich speziell zu danken, weil sie für dieses Buch mehr getan haben, als ich erwarten durfte. Um nur die wichtigsten zu nennen: David R. Phillips, der mir großzügigerweise alle Fuermann-Photos, die sich seit 1972 in seinem Besitz befinden, zur Verfügung stellte; Tim Samuelson, der mir wichtige Hinweise und ein Gefühl für den Stoff gab; Bruno Maurer, der das Manuskript las; Sandra Brandeberry, die die Übersetzung besorgte. Dank Professor Werner Oechslin wurde die Arbeit vom Institut für Geschichte und Theorie der Architektur (gta) der Eidgenössischen Technischen Hochschule Zürich unterstützt.

Very few of the buildings which Louis Sullivan created, alone or along with his partner Dankmar Adler, have survived economic pressures and remain intact. Many of them, however, have been superbly documented, first of all thanks to Henry Fuermann, who, along with his sons Leon and Clarence, photographed Sullivan's buildings shortly after their completion. In all probability the photographs were made chiefly by Clarence. Recognition is also due to Richard Nickel, who resisted the destruction of the buildings, tragically losing his life in the rubble of the demolished Chicago Stock Exchange Building by Adler & Sullivan.

I owe a special debt of gratitude to a number of people who have done more for the present work than I could have expected. To name only the most important of them: David R. Phillips, who generously made available to me all the Fuermann photographs in his possession since 1972; Tim Samuelson, who gave me some valuable hints and deepened my awareness of the material; Bruno Maurer, who read the manuscript; Sandra Brandeberry, who did the translation. Thanks to Professor Werner Oechslin, the work received the support of the Institute for the History and Theory of Architecture (gta) at the Swiss Federal Institute of Technology in Zurich.

Louis H. Sullivan, Dezember 1876.
Louis H. Sullivan, December 1876.

«Sullivan gegen die Welt»
"Sullivan against the World"

Man hat Sullivan «Vater der modernen Architektur», «Vater des Funktionalismus», «Vater des Wolkenkratzers» genannt; aber man hat mit seinem Namen auch einen Stil bezeichnet, der sich durch exzessive Ornamente auszeichnet: «ein kompliziertes Verweben von linear-geometrischen Formen mit stilisierten Blättern zu einem symmetrischen Muster» (Blumenson 1977, S. 65). Dieselbe Ungereimtheit begegnet einem, wenn man Sullivans berühmtes Diktum «form follows function» auf die von ihm errichteten Bauten bezieht. Die mit Ornamenten überladenen Fassaden scheinen aufzuzeigen, daß ihr Entwerfer noch nicht begriffen hat, was er so brillant in Worte fassen konnte. So zieht sich eine Kluft zwischen progressiven und traditionellen Aspekten durch das Werk von Sullivan. Er gilt deshalb als ein Architekt, der sich wohl auf dem rechten Pfad (der Moderne) befand, doch von seinen «Gewohnheitssünden» – oder sollte man in Anlehnung an Adolf Loos sagen: Gewohnheitsverbrechen? – noch nicht ganz losgekommen ist.

Ob es nun seine Tragik oder seine Größe ausmacht, Tatsache ist, daß Sullivan, wie kaum ein anderer Architekt seiner Zeit, um die Einheit eines Bauwerks gerungen hat. Er suchte nach einer Regel, die keine Ausnahme kennt. Dieser einheitliche Baugedanke lief jedoch weder auf einen rigorosen Ausdruck der Konstruktion noch auf eine dekorierte Konstruktion hinaus. Er beruht weder auf klassischen Idealen noch auf der Unterordnung unter konstruktive Aspekte. Die Einheit, wie sie Sullivan verstand, setzt hingegen den Bruch zwischen dem strukturellen System und der formalen Hülle voraus und basiert auf neuen poetischen Strategien der Vermittlung zwischen diesen unabhängig gewordenen Aspekten eines Bauwerks. Im Unterschied zu Loos sah Sullivan die Entwicklung der Architektur nicht als «gleichbedeutend mit dem entfernen des ornaments» (Loos 1908, S. 277), sondern in der Möglichkeit, jedem Bau, unabhängig von Stilklaubereien, einen individuellen Ausdruck zu geben.

Sullivan has been called the "father of modern architecture", "father of functionalism", and "father of the skyscraper", yet his name has also been used to denote a style that is marked by excessive ornament: "an intricate weaving of linear and geometric forms with stylized foliage in a symmetrical pattern" (Blumenson 1977, p. 65). The same inconsistency is apparent when one tries to apply Sullivan's famous dictum "form follows function" to his buildings. The façades covered in ornament seem to indicate that their designer failed to grasp that which he so brilliantly formulated in words. This tension between the progressive and the traditional pervades Sullivan's entire œuvre. He is considered, therefore, an architect who was no doubt on the "right" track (toward the modern), yet he never quite freed himself from his "habitual sins" – or to borrow from the Viennese modernist, Adolf Loos, one could say: habitual crimes.

Whether it constitutes his tragedy or his genius, the fact remains that Sullivan, like scarcely any other architect of his time, strove for the idea of a building as a formal unity. He was in search of a rule that admitted no exception. This notion led neither to a rigorous expression of structure nor to a decorated structure. It was neither based on classical ideals nor on subordination to structural principles. Unity, as Sullivan understood it, presumes, rather, a split between the structural system and the formalistic exterior shell. Thus, this unity was based on new poetic strategies of mediation between these two aspects of a building. Contrary to Loos, Sullivan did not view the development of architecture as "synonymous with the removal of ornament" (Loos 1908, p. 277) but rather, in the possibility of expressing each building individually, independent of questions of historical style.

In the following essay, an attempt will be made to establish a correlation between Sullivan's intentions (as stated in his writings) and his buildings. The focus will be primar-

Im folgenden wird zum einen versucht, Sullivans Intentionen, die er schriftlich darlegte, mit dem Gebauten in Beziehung zu bringen. Das Augenmerk liegt dabei hauptsächlich auf der Beziehung zwischen Konstruktion und Dekoration. Zweitens sollen die verschiedenen Werkphasen als eine Abfolge behandelt werden, die durch die kontinuierliche Suche nach Lösungen für ein zentrales architektonisches Problem miteinander verbunden sind. Es handelt sich dabei erneut um das Verhältnis von Konstruktion und Dekoration, welches wie ein roter Faden die ersten Bauten im romantischen Stil, die richardsonesken Bauten, die berühmten Hochhäuser und mondänen Warenhäuser mit den «verrückten» Bankgebäuden verbindet.

Erste Begegnungen mit Architektur

Am 3. September 1856 kam Louis Henry als zweites Kind von Andrienne, geborene List, und Patrick Sullivan in Boston, Massachusetts, zur Welt. Seine Mutter stammte aus Genf, sein Vater war Ire. Die Familie lebte von den Einkünften einer Tanzschule, die während der Sommersaison auch außerhalb von Boston geführt wurde. Deshalb hielt sich Louis meistens bei seinen Großeltern mütterlicherseits auf, die 1861 auf eine kleine Farm in South Reading umzogen.

1864 wurde Louis in Boston eingeschult, nachdem er sich zuvor in South Reading erfolgreich dagegen zu wehren vermochte. Seine Abneigung gegen Lehrer und Schule, ein «Gefängnis für Kinder», blieb, und er maß den einschlägigen Erfahrungen in seinen Lebenserinnerungen keine große Bedeutung zu. Allerdings erzählt er aus dieser Zeit von zwei Erlebnissen, die beide hinsichtlich seiner späteren Karriere bedeutungsvoll sind.

Den Sommer 1863 verbrachte Louis zusammen mit seiner Familie in Newburyport (Sullivan, 1922/24, S. 82). Bei einem Picknick am Merrimac schlich er sich davon und durchstöberte alleine das Dickicht am Ufer. Plötzlich erblickte er durch die Blätter etwas Dunkles, das ihm Angst machte. Er ging trotzdem weiter, bis das ganze, furchterregende Gebilde groß vor ihm stand. Er hielt es für ein lebendiges Monster, das ihn im Nu verschlingen würde. Er rief um Hilfe, und der Vater erklärte ihm, was eine Brücke ist und wozu die beiden hohen steinernen Türme und das lange Band, das an schweren Ketten hängt, nützlich sind. Auf dem Rückweg drehte sich Louis voll Bewunderung

ily on the inter-relationship between structure and ornament. Secondly, the different stages of his professional career will be treated as a progression in the ongoing search for solutions to a central architectonic problem, i. e. the relationship between structure and ornament. This has been a leitmotif throughout Sullivan's work – from the early Romanesque style and the Richardsonesque buildings to the famous tall office buildings, the chic department stores, and finally the "crazy" banks.

First Encounter with Architecture

Louis Henry was born the second of two sons to Andrienne née List and Patrick Sullivan on September 3, 1856 in Boston, Massachusetts. His mother, a French-Swiss originally from Geneva, and his father, an Irishman, earned their livelihood through a dance academy which operated during the summer in and around Boston. Louis spent most of the summers of his youth with his maternal grandparents who had lived on a small farm in South Reading since 1861.

In 1864 Louis was finally sent to school in Boston, after having successfully resisted it in South Reading. However, he retained this abhorrence of teachers and school, "prisons for children", throughout his life. Although he did not attach much importance to these early experiences in his memoirs, he does relate two events from his childhood that would have a great impact on his future career.

The first one was in 1863 when Louis spent the summer with his family in Newburyport where his father had established a summer school of dancing (Sullivan 1922/24, p. 82). During a picnic on the Merrimac, he slipped away and wandered alone through a thicket on the bank of the river. Suddenly he saw something dark amidst the foliage which frightened him. Nevertheless, he continued on until the horrible thing loomed up in front of him. He thought the thing was a monster that would gobble him up any second. He cried out for his father who told him that the "monster" was just a bridge. After explaining the purpose of the two high stone towers and the long band hanging from heavy chains, Louis was fascinated. On the way back, he turned around full of amazement overwhelmed by the fact that man can create something so magnificent.

um, überwältigt vom Gefühl, daß der Mensch so etwas Großartiges schaffen kann.

Wenig später beobachtete Louis vor einem Bauplatz in Boston einen würdevollen Herrn, der gerade in einer Kutsche den Ort verließ. Er erkundigte sich beim Vorarbeiter über diesen Mann und erfuhr, daß dies der Architekt des Bauwerks sei und daß ein Architekt die Aufteilung der Räume festlege und ein Bild des Äußeren zeichne, welches er «aus seinem Kopf heraus erschaffe» (Sullivan 1922/23, S. 119/120). Der junge Sullivan entschied sich auf der Stelle, selbst auch ein solcher Architekt zu werden und Gebäude aus seinem Kopf heraus zu erschaffen. Doch der Bauarbeiter zeigte sich skeptisch und brachte Bedenken vor, die Sullivan wahrscheinlich sein Leben lang immer wieder zu hören bekam: Er sehe nicht so aus, als sei er sehr praktisch begabt mit seinem träumerischen Blick.

1870 trat Louis in die English High School ein, wo im ersten Jahr Moses Woolson unterrichtete. Dieser machte seine Schüler mit dem berühmten Botaniker Asa Gray, der an der nahen Harvard University lehrte, bekannt und empfahl ihnen das Buch des französischen Philosophen Hippolyte Taine über englische Literatur, welches gerade in englischer Übersetzung erschienen war. Sullivan bezog sich zeit seines Lebens immer wieder auf Werke der beiden, und Woolson ist der einzige Lehrer, den er als Autorität akzeptierte.

Nach einem weiteren Jahr an der English High School bestand Sullivan die Aufnahmeprüfung am «Massachusetts Institute of Technology» (MIT) und begann dort mit dem Architekturstudium. Das «Tech» ist die älteste Architekturschule Amerikas, die seit ihrer Gründung im Jahre 1865 von William R. Ware (1832–1915) geleitet wurde. Ware hatte zuvor im New Yorker Büro von Richard M. Hunt (1827–1895), dem ersten amerikanischen Architekten, der an der École des Beaux-Arts in Paris studierte, gearbeitet. Dort traf er Henry van Brunt (1832–1903), mit dem er von 1863 bis 1881 ein Architekturbüro in Boston führte. Während die beiden Partner den Stil ihrer Bauten in eklektizistischer Manier flexibel Bauprogrammen und Zeitgeschmack anpaßten, bezogen sie in ihren theoretischen Arbeiten diametral entgegengesetzte Positionen. Ware orientierte sich bei seinen Kursen am «Tech» am Vorbild der Beaux-Arts. Er machte 1871 einen Beaux-Arts-Absolventen, Eugène Létang, der bei Emile Vaudremer studiert hatte, zu seinem Assistenten. Nach «Greek Ornament» im Jahre 1878 veröffentlichte er 1901 als

The second experience followed shortly after in Boston. Louis noticed a gentleman come out of a building at a construction site and enter his carriage. Asking a foreman about this man, he found out that he was the architect of the building – the person who determines the arrangement of the rooms and draws pictures of how the exterior of the building should look. Louis made up his mind then and there to become an architect and make beautiful buildings "out of his head" (Sullivan 1922/23, pp. 119/120). Yet the foreman seemed skeptical, expressing doubts which Sullivan probably heard time and time again: He did not look very practical with that "far-away look in yer [sic] eyes".

In 1870 Louis entered the Boston English High School where he was taught by Moses Woolson, the only teacher whose authority Sullivan ever accepted. He introduced his students to the work of the famous botanist Asa Gray, who taught at the near-by Harvard University, recommending also the book on English literature by Hippolyte Taine, the nineteenth-century French critic and philosopher of art, which had just appeared in English translation. Throughout his life, Sullivan consulted works by both these authors.

After completing one more year at the English High School, Sullivan passed the entrance exam for MIT, the Massachusetts Institute of Technology. Founded in 1865, "Tech" was the first architecture school in America. Sullivan enrolled in the architecture course taught by Professor William R. Ware (1832–1915) who had been director of "Tech" since its establishment in 1865. Ware had previously worked in the New York office of Richard M. Hunt (1827–95), the first American architect to study at the Ecole des Beaux-Arts in Paris. There he met Henry van Brunt (1832–1903) with whom he later formed the architectural firm of Ware and Van Brunt of Boston which they ran from 1863 to 1881. Although both partners adapted the style of their buildings in an eclectic manner to flexible architectural programs and contemporary taste, on other architectural issues, however, they were diametrically opposed: Ware oriented his courses at "Tech" to classical rules of architecture in accordance with the Beaux-Arts tradition. In 1871 he engaged Eugène Létang as his assistant, a recent Beaux-Arts graduate who had studied at the Atelier Vaudremer. After publishing "Greek Ornament" in 1878, Ware published the cumulative sum of all his teachings in 1901 under the title of "The American Vignola". In 1875, van Brunt, on

Summe seiner Lehre der klassischen Regeln der Architektur «The American Vignola». Van Brunt seinerseits übersetzte und veröffentlichte 1875 die beiden Bände der «Entretiens sur l'architecture» (1863, 1872) von Eugène-Emmanuel Viollet-le-Duc, der der offiziellen klassischen Lehre an der Beaux-Arts sehr ablehnend gegenüberstand. Seine Einführung in das Werk des französischen Theoretikers verrät genaue Kenntnisse der Architekturdebatten an der Beaux-Arts. Sullivan erwarb dieses Werk später für seine Bibliothek.

Über die Zeit am «Tech» verliert Sullivan in seinen Aufzeichnungen nur wenige Worte, die zudem gegen Lehrer und Ausbildungssystem gerichtet sind. Immerhin lernte er dort, die fünf klassischen Säulenordnungen nach Vorlagen perfekt abzuzeichnen (Abbildung 1). Die Indoktrination aus zweiter Hand wollte ihm jedoch nicht gefallen, und so entschloß er sich, bereits nach einem Jahr, die Theorien dort zu studieren, von wo sie herkamen: an der École des Beaux-Arts in Paris. Den makabren Eindruck, den ihm der «Friedhof der Ordnungen» (Sullivan 1922/23, S. 189) machte, hoffte er in der Zentrale der klassischen Theorie zu überwinden.

Sullivan reiste zunächst nach New York, wo er den führenden Architekten Amerikas, Richard M. Hunt, auf-

the other hand, translated and published both volumes of "Entretiens sur l'architecture" (1863, 1872) by Eugène-Emmanuel Viollet-le-Duc, one of the major critics of the official teachings of the Beaux-Arts. Van Brunt's introduction reveals an in-depth knowledge of Viollet's theories as well as the Beaux-Arts debates. Sullivan later acquired this work for his library.

Sullivan said very little in his memoirs about the time he spent at MIT. Most of his comments were, however, directed against teachers and the educational system. Nevertheless, at "Tech" he did learn to draw expertly the five orders of classical columns (Illustration 1). However, second-hand indoctrination did not suit Sullivan, so after only a year he decided to study the theories where they originated: at the Ecole des Beaux-Arts in Paris. At the "headquarters" of classical theory, he hoped to overcome the macabre impression that the "cemetery of orders" (Sullivan 1922/23, p. 189) had made upon him.

On his way to Paris, Sullivan stopped off in New York to meet the leading architect in America, Richard M. Hunt. It seems likely that he intended to work for him, but he had to be content with good advice for Paris.

In June 1873, Sullivan went to Philadelphia where he was

2 Furness & Hewitt:
Guarantee Trust and Safe
Deposit Company Building,
Philadelphia, 1873–75.

2 *Furness & Hewitt:*
Guarantee Trust and Safe
Deposit Company Building,
Philadelphia, 1873–75.

suchte. Es ist anzunehmen, daß er bei ihm arbeiten wollte, um zunächst einige praktische Erfahrungen zu erwerben, doch mußte er sich mit guten Ratschlägen für Paris begnügen.

Die nächste Etappe war Philadelphia, wo Sullivan von Frank Furness (1839–1912) im Juni 1873 angestellt wurde. Furness hatte den Ruf eines «großen wilden Mannes der amerikanischen Architektur». Er faszinierte Sullivan vor allem, weil er tatsächlich Gebäude «aus seinem Kopf heraus erschuf» (Sullivan 1922/23, S. 193). Zudem hat ihn wohl auch das kulturelle Klima der Stadt, das von der Familie Furness wesentlich geprägt wurde, interessiert. Der Vater von Frank Furness war ein lebenslanger Freund von Ralph Emerson und las wie alle Transzendentalisten begeistert Goethe und Schiller. Frank Furness selbst war mit der zeitgenössischen Kunst und Architektur in England und Frankreich bestens vertraut. Als Quellen dienten ihm einerseits das Büro von Hunt, wo er zwischen 1851 und 1865 mit Unterbrechungen gearbeitet hatte, andererseits auch Philadelphias Intellektuellenzeitschrift «Penn Monthly», in der regelmäßig Berichte über Ruskin, Viollet-le-Duc und die französischen Romantiker erschienen. Als Hauptwerk von Furness gilt das Gebäude der Pennsylvania Academy of Fine Arts, das gerade im Bau war, als Sullivan in Philadelphia weilte. Doch dieser erwähnt in der Autobiographie namentlich nur den Neubau einer Bank an der Chestnut Street, für welche er Pläne gezeichnet hatte (Abbildung 2; Sullivan 1922/23, S. 193). Im Herbst 1873 wurde er infolge einer anhaltenden wirtschaftlichen Depression, die auch die Auftrags-

hired by Frank Furness (1839–1912), the "great wild man of American architecture". Sullivan was fascinated by Furness, particularly because he really did "make buildings out of his head" (Sullivan 1922/23, p. 193). In addition, he was interested in the cultural climate of the city which was to a large extent influenced by the Furness family. Frank Furness' father was a lifelong friend of Ralph Emerson and, like all transcendentalists, enthusiastically read Goethe and Schiller. Frank Furness himself was well acquainted with contemporary art and architecture in both England and France. His sources included Hunt's office, where he had worked periodically between 1851 and 1865, as well as Philadelphia's intellectual journal, "Penn Monthly", in which articles on Ruskin, Viollet-le-Duc, and the French Romantics regularly appeared. Although the Pennsylvania Academy of Fine Arts, considered the most important work of Furness, was under construction while Sullivan was in Philadelphia, in his autobiography he only mentions drawing up the plans for a new bank building on Chestnut Street (Illustration 2; Sullivan 1922/23, p. 193). Due to the Panic of 1873, which caused a drastic decline in the number of commissions at Furness & Hewitt, they were forced to lay Sullivan off after only a few short months.

Apparently still not quite ready for the big jump into the "headquarters" of architecture, in 1873 Sullivan arrived in Chicago, where his parents had lived since 1868. The city appealed to him immediately: "This is the place for me!" (Sullivan 1924, p. 197). After the Great Fire of 1871, which destroyed nearly the entire city center,

3 Chicago, Ecke La Salle und
Lake Streets, 1875.

3 Chicago, Corner La Salle
and Lake Streets, 1875.

lage von Furness & Hewitt drastisch verschlechterte, entlassen.

Offensichlich noch immer nicht zum großen Sprung ins «Hauptquartier» der Architektur bereit, traf Sullivan vor dem Thanksgiving Day 1873 in Chicago ein, wo seine Eltern seit 1868 lebten. Die Stadt gefiel ihm auf Anhieb: «Das ist der Ort für mich!» (Sullivan 1924, S. 197) Nach dem katastrophalen Brand von 1871, der praktisch das ganze Zentrum zerstörte, brach eine Euphorie aus, als wäre alles nur eine gottgeschickte Prüfung gewesen, die die Stadt nun meistern mußte, um an die Spitze aller Städte zu gelangen (Abbildung 3; Zukowsky 1987, S. 27). Bereits vor dem Brand war Chicago eine florierende Stadt: Hier waren der weltweit größte Getreidemarkt, der größte Holzmarkt, die größten Schlachthöfe angesiedelt. Die «Jetzt-erst-recht»-Stimmung riß Sullivan mit, und es ist naheliegend, daß er unter diesen Umständen als Architekt jede Menge Arbeit erwarten durfte. Allerdings verursachte die wirtschaftliche Depression auch in Chicago einen momentanen Rückgang der Aufträge.

Sullivan meldete sich im Büro von William Le Baron Jenney (1832–1907), weil ihm in den Straßen Chicagos dessen Bauten am interessantesten schienen, und wurde prompt angestellt. Jenney hatte an der École Centrale des Arts et Manufactures in Paris studiert. Er spielte für die Entwicklung der modernen Architektur in Chicago jene Rolle, die Peter Behrens zu Anfang des 20. Jahrhunderts in Berlin innehatte. So wie dort die späteren Meister der Modernen Architektur – Le Corbusier, Mies van der Rohe

euphoria broke out, as if this were a challenge from God which the city must overcome in order to become the city of all cities (Illustration 3; Zukowsky 1987, p. 27). Even before the fire, Chicago was a flourishing city: This was the home of the world's largest grain market, the largest timber industry as well as the largest slaughter houses. Sullivan was naturally infected by this "now-more-than-ever" mood. Under these circumstances architects could normally expect a lot of work. Unfortunately, the ongoing economic depression had also caused a temporary decline in commissions in Chicago.

Sullivan then applied for a position at the office of William Le Baron Jenney (1832–1907) in Chicago, where he was hired immediately. Jenney, who had studied at the Ecole Centrale des Arts et Manufactures in Paris, played the same role in the development of modern architecture in Chicago as Peter Behrens did in Berlin at the beginning of the 20th century: Just as those who would later become the masters of modern architecture – Le Corbusier, Mies van der Rohe, and Gropius – succeeded each other as employees in Behrens' office, so it was with Jenney in Chicago. Many of the architects who worked for him would later make a name for themselves in the "Chicago School of Architecture": Daniel H. Burnham, John W. Root, William Holabird, and, contemporaneously with Sullivan, Martin Roche. In particular, however, Sullivan met John Edelmann, Jenney's office foreman, who was to become his mentor. He was an important source of ideas for Sullivan as well as the first person with whom he dis-

und Gropius – einander als Angestellte ablösten, so arbeiteten hier viele jener Architekten, die sich in den achtziger Jahren innerhalb der «Chicago School of Architecture» einen Namen machen sollten: Daniel H. Burnham, John W. Root, William Holabird und, gleichzeitig mit Sullivan, Martin Roche. Insbesondere aber Jenneys Bürovorsteher, John Edelmann, war für ihn ein wichtiger Gesprächspartner und der erste, mit dem er theoretische Probleme der Architektur diskutierte. Der Kontakt zwischen beiden brach auch während Sullivans Aufenthalt in Paris nicht ab.

Im Hauptquartier der Architektur

Als Sullivan im Sommer 1874 in Paris ankam, war die École des Beaux-Arts weltweit die führende Schule für Architektur. Absolventen der Schule nahmen die Schlüsselpositionen ihres Berufsstandes ein – nicht nur in Frankreich, auch anderswo: Man denke etwa an Richard M. Hunt in New York. Nirgends gab es eine weitere Institution, wo mit der gleichen Autorität das für Architekten als notwendig erachtete Wissen verbreitet worden wäre.

Die École des Beaux-Arts ging aus der 1671 gegründeten Académie royale d'architecture hervor, die 1793 durch den revolutionären Nationalkonvent geschlossen wurde, um zwei Jahre später als «École des Beaux-Arts» mit praktisch identischen Strukturen wieder eröffnet zu werden. Die Schule war von Anfang an im wesentlichen ein Trainingslager für Bewerber um den jährlich ausgeschriebenen «Grand Prix de Rome». Neben der Aussicht auf eine glänzende Karriere durfte der Sieger sich während fünf Jahren auf Kosten des französischen Staates als Pensionär der Villa Medici in Rom aufhalten. Wer am Wettbewerb teilnehmen wollte, mußte eine Zulassungsprüfung in den Fächern Zeichnen, Komposition, Mathematik und Geschichte erfolgreich hinter sich gebracht haben. In den Ateliers, die ihm zur Auswahl standen, konnte er an den monatlich ausgeschriebenen Wettbewerben («concours d'émulation») teilnehmen, um sich so für den Grand Prix vorzubereiten.

Die Geschichte der École des Beaux-Arts im 19. Jahrhundert ist gekennzeichnet von Angriffen auf die klassizistische Position, an der unter andern und insbesondere der sehr einflußreiche «secrétaire perpétuel» der Akademie von 1816–1839, Antoine-Chrisostome Quatremère de

cussed theoretical problems of architecture. They kept in touch even while Sullivan was in Paris.

At the Headquarters of Architecture

When Sullivan arrived in Paris in 1874, the Ecole des Beaux Arts was the world's leading intellectual center of architecture. Graduates of the school filled key positions in their field – not only in France, but throughout the world: Richard M. Hunt in New York immediately comes to mind. Nowhere in the world was there a comparable institution where the knowledge deemed necessary for the study of architecture was accumulated so systematically and disseminated with such an air of authority.

The Ecole des Beaux-Arts was an offshoot of the Académie Royale d'Architecture founded in 1671. Although closed in 1793 by the revolutionary National Assembly, it was reopened with virtually the same structure two years later and renamed the "Ecole des Beaux-Arts". From the very beginning, the school was a training camp for participants in the annual "Grand Prix de Rome". Along with prospects for a brilliant career, the winner was invited to spend five years at the expense of the French government at the Villa Medici in Rome. In order to be admitted to the competition, all students had first to pass an exam in the following subjects: drawing, composition, mathematics, and history. Then they could enter one of the ateliers where they could take part in monthly competitions ("concours d'émulation") in order to accumulate enough points to register for the "Grand Prix".

The history of the Ecole des Beaux-Arts during the 19th century is marked by opposition to the classical tradition posited by, among others, the very influential Antoine-Chrisostome Quatremère de Quincy who was "secrétaire perpétuel" of the Académie Royale d'Architecture between 1816 and 1839. According to Quincy, only a small number of buildings erected during the reign of the Roman Emperor Augustus earned the right to serve as models for future generations because they alone completely embodied the classical ideal that art should imitate nature. The winners of the "Grand Prix" were required to adhere to the study of classical Roman antiquity in their obligatory projects.

Criticism of classical idealism came from the so-called "Romantic School" which had split off into two direc-

4 Henri Labrouste:
Bibliothèque Sainte-
Geneviève, Paris, 1838–51.

4 Henri Labrouste:
Bibliothèque Sainte-
Geneviève, Paris, 1838–51.

Quincy, festhielt. Ihm zufolge galt nur für wenige Bauwerke aus der Zeit des römischen Kaisers Augustus, daß die Gesetze der Natur in ihnen vollkommen nachgeahmt waren und daß sie sich somit das Recht erworben hatten, für immer als Vorbilder zu dienen. Die Grand-Prix-Gewinner wurden angewiesen, sich in ihren obligatorischen Arbeiten an das Studium der klassischen römischen Antike zu halten.

Die Kritik am klassizistischen Idealismus kam von der sogenannten «Romantischen Schule», die sich in eine neu-griechische und eine neu-gotische Richtung aufteilte. Erstere wurde angeführt von Duban, Duc, Labrouste und Vaudoyer, alles Gewinner des Grand Prix, die sich um 1826 in Rom zu einer Art konspirativem Zirkel zusammenschlossen. Insbesondere Labroustes letzter Bericht an die Akademie von 1828 über die Ruinen der dorischen Tempel von Paestum löste in Paris einen Skandal aus. Die Abweichungen von den klassischen Regeln, die die peinlich genaue Aufnahme dieses massigen Bauwerks zutage förderten, dienten als Einstieg, den griechischen Geist neu zu beleben und – statt an absoluten Regeln festzuhalten – gerade aufgrund präziserer Kenntnisse sich eine größere Freiheit in der eigenen Konzeption vorzubehalten. Die Bibliothek Sainte-Geneviève in Paris (Abbildung 4) ist ein Hauptwerk der neu-griechischen Richtung. Labrouste führte hier insbesondere vor, was es bedeutet, ein Bauwerk – im Sinne des griechischen Geistes – mit eigenem Stil, eigenem Charakter und eigenen Formen entsprechend seinem Zwecke auszustatten (vergleiche Levine 1977).

Auch den Neu-Gotikern, deren wichtigster Protagonist und Theoretiker in Frankreich Eugène Viollet-le-Duc war, ging es darum, die Beziehung zwischen Form und Bedeutung gegenüber den Klassizisten neu zu definieren. Sich vor allem auf einheimische Traditionen berufend, setzten

tions: Néo-grec and Gothic Revival. The Néo-grecs were led by Duban, Duc, Labrouste and Vaudoyer, all former winners of the "Grand Prix", who had formed a kind of conspiratorial circle in Rome in 1826. In particular, Labrouste's last report presented to the Academy in 1828 on the ruins of the doric Temple of Paestum caused a scandal in Paris. His rigorous analysis of this colossal structure revealed a departure from classical rules. This new and more accurate information triggered a rejuvenation of the classical Greek spirit because it allowed for greater freedom in individual expression as opposed to rigidly adhering to absolute rules. The Ste. Geneviève Library in Paris (Illustration 4) is considered the finest example of a building in the Néo-grec style. Here Labrouste demonstrates specifically what it means – in accordance with the ancient Greek spirit – to endow a structure with a unique and individual style, character and forms according to its particular purpose (cf.: Levine 1977).

The Gothic Revivalists, whose most important spokesman and theoretician in France was Viollet-le-Duc, were, like the Néo-grecs, also interested in redefining the relationship between form and meaning. By referring to local traditions in France, they attempted to give the material a form which seemed appropriate to its specific physical properties.

Neither Labrouste nor Viollet-le-Duc were able to gain acceptance within the Ecole des Beaux-Arts. However, by the time Sullivan arrived in Paris in the summer of 1874, a second less radical generation of the Romantic School had begun to take hold. With Julien Guadet, they even occupied one of the three official ateliers. Of all the patrons of the "atelier libre", André, Coquart and Questel were the closest to the Néo-grecs. Vaudremer, on the other hand, was considered one of the "apostles of Viollet-le-Duc". Even the "pensionnaires" in Rome no longer

sie beim Material an und versuchten, diesem jeweils jene Form zu geben, die ihm von seinen spezifischen Eigenschaften her angemessen schien.

Weder Labrouste noch Viollet-le-Duc hatten sich innerhalb der École des Beaux-Arts durchzusetzen vermocht. Doch als Sullivan im Sommer 1874 nach Paris kam, hatte sich inzwischen eine zweite, weniger radikale Generation der Romantischen Schule etabliert. Diese besetzte mit Julien Guadet gar eines der drei offiziellen Ateliers. Von den Patrons der «freien Ateliers» standen André, Coquart und Questel den Neu-Griechen nahe, während Vaudremer zu den «Aposteln von Viollet-le-Duc» zählte. Auch die Pensionäre in Rom ließen sich in ihren Studien längst nicht mehr auf Ruinen der klassischen Antike einschränken, sondern drangen immer weiter nach Osten vor, zuerst nach Griechenland, später bis ins Zweistromland.

Wie die meisten seiner amerikanischen Kommilitonen, die vom «Tech» an die Beaux-Arts wechselten, schrieb sich Sullivan nach erfolgreich bestandener Aufnahmeprüfung im freien Atelier von Emile Vaudremer (1829–1914) ein. Schon nach wenigen Monaten unterbrach er jedoch seine Arbeit und reiste nach Italien. Ziel war Rom, wo er sich erstaunlicherweise nur drei Tage aufhielt, zwei davon allein in der Sixtinischen Kapelle vor den berühmten Fresken von Michelangelo. Dann kehrte er via Florenz, wo er sechs Wochen blieb, nach Paris zurück. Über eine Beteiligung Sullivans an einem der monatlichen Wettbewerbe ist nichts bekannt. Erhalten geblieben sind aus jener Zeit nur Zeichnungen, die er an John Edelmann in Chicago schickte. Bereits im Mai 1875 schloß Sullivan das Kapitel der akademischen Ausbildung für immer ab und kehrte nach Chicago zurück.

In seiner Autobiographie berichtet Sullivan weniger von der Beaux-Arts selbst, als vielmehr von Nebenschauplätzen wie der Vorbereitung für die mathematische Aufnahmeprüfung bei Monsieur Clopet. Dessen Beharren auf Lösungen, die ohne Ausnahme gültig sind, greift er sofort auf und nimmt sich vor, auch für das Gebiet der Architektur nach Regeln ohne Ausnahme («no exception») zu suchen. Seinen frühzeitigen Weggang aus Paris begründet er damit, daß die Beaux-Arts von der Theorie der Zeichnung beherrscht sei, die zwar zu brillanten Resultaten führe, jedoch abstrakt und ohne Bezug zur Realität bleibe.

Trotzdem kann die Bedeutung der École des Beaux-Arts für Sullivan kaum unterschätzt werden. Die Beaux-Arts

restricted themselves in their studies to the ruins of classical antiquity, but began to shift their focus further east, first to Greece, then to Mesopotamia.

After passing the entrance exam, Sullivan, like most of the American architecture students who transferred from "Tech" to the Beaux-Arts, registered at the "atelier libre" of Emile Vaudremer (1829–1914). However, he interrupted his studies only a few months later to travel to Italy. Although his goal was to visit Rome, he surprisingly spent only three days there, two of them in the Sistine Chapel gazing at the famous frescoes of Michelangelo. Before returning to Paris, he spent six weeks in Florence. Whether or not Sullivan participated in one of the monthly competitions while he was in Paris is unknown. All that has survived from this time are a few drawings which Sullivan had sent to John Edelmann in Chicago.

In his autobiography, Sullivan focuses less on the Beaux-Arts itself and more on things of seemingly lesser importance, such as the preparation for the entrance exam in mathematics at Monsieur Clopet's. Yet Clopet's insistence on solutions which are "such as to admit of no exception" (Sullivan 1922/23, p. 312) appealed to Sullivan immediately. He decided to search for rules with "no exception" in architecture – a search that would prove to have a great impact on his later career and the development of his "Idea". Nevertheless, in May 1875, only a year after arriving in Paris, Sullivan returned to Chicago, putting an abrupt end to his academic education. The reason for his rather premature departure from Paris was that the Beaux-Arts, according to Sullivan, was too dominated by drawing theory which, although leading to brilliant results, remained abstract and disconnected from reality.

Yet the significance of the Beaux-Arts for Sullivan can scarcely be underestimated. By 1874, the Beaux-Arts was no longer the cradle of classical ideas, a position it had enjoyed since the beginning of the nineteenth century. The intellectual climate at the Beaux-Arts was marked by a search for new architectonic concepts. Vaudremer, Sullivan's patron in Paris, among others, contributed to this by trying to synthesize classical and medieval theories, two artistic styles which were considered unreconcilable up to that time (Illustration 5). Similarly, the lectures of Hippolyte Taine, Professor of Art History, contributed to this new direction. Sullivan had read Taine's most important

5 Emile Vaudremer: Saint-
Pierre-de-Montrouge, Paris,
1864–72.

5 Emile Vaudremer: Saint-
Pierre-de-Montrouge, Paris
1864–72.

war um 1874 nicht mehr der Hort klassischer Ideale wie zu Beginn des 19. Jahrhunderts. Ihr geistiges Klima war von der Suche nach neuen architektonischen Konzepten geprägt. Dazu leistete unter andern Vaudremer, Sullivans Patron, einen Beitrag, indem er eine Synthese aus klassischer und mittelalterlicher Auffassung versuchte, aus zwei künstlerischen Tendenzen mithin, die zuvor als unvereinbar galten (Abbildung 5). Ebenso gehörten die Vorlesungen des Professors für Kunstgeschichte, Hippolyte Taine, zu diesem Umfeld. Sullivan hatte dessen Hauptwerk «Philosophie de l'art» in Paris gelesen und hörte wahrscheinlich auch die Vorlesungen im «Hémicycle». Taine entwickelte eine evolutionistische Sicht der Kulturgeschichte, in Analogie zu naturwissenschaftlichen Theorien von Spencer und Darwin, wonach sich die Entwicklung künstlerischer Formen als Anpassung an vorliegende Ursachen und als Entwicklung auf den optimalen Ausdruck hin verstehen läßt. Kunst ist in diesem Zusammenhang kein abgehobenes Spiel der Imagination, sondern ein Transskript der «condition morale» (Rasse, Milieu, Zeit). Einzig der Künstler ist in der Lage, die Be-

work, "Philosophie de l'art", in Paris and probably also heard the lectures in the "Hémicycle". Taine's view of cultural history was analogous to the evolutionary theories of Spencer and Darwin. The development of artistic forms may be understood as an adaptation to existing causes which is an integral part in the process of evolution toward optimal expression. In this context, art is not an abstract game of imagination but a transcript of the "condition morale" (race, social milieu, era). According to Taine, only the artist can reveal the spirit of a nation, of a generation, or an era; he creates those works that have the most expressive value within a society. Each great work of art is, first and foremost, an expression of a specific culture; each new problem must find its own unique style and form.

Although he taught at the nearby Ecole des Arts Décoratifs, Victor-Marie Ruprich-Robert was another proponent of that new direction whose influence was being felt within the Ecole des Beaux-Arts while Sullivan was there. Ruprich-Robert's "Flore ornementale", a volume of plates published in various installments between 1866

6 Victor-Marie Ruprich-Robert: Flore ornementale, Paris,
1866–76, Tafel 108.
6 Victor-Marie Ruprich-Robert: Flore ornementale, Paris,
1866–76, plate 108.

7 Louis H. Sullivan: Kopie nach Ruprich-Robert, um 1875.
7 Louis H. Sullivan: Copy from Ruprich-Robert, about 1875.

findlichkeit einer Nation, einer Epoche zu enthüllen, er
schafft – immer nach Taine – jene Werke mit dem höch-
sten Ausdruckswert innerhalb einer Gesellschaft. Jedes
große Kunstwerk ist so zunächst einmal Ausdruck einer
bestimmten Kultur; jedes neue Problem muß seinen eigenen Stil und seine eigene Form finden.

Des weiteren ist auch Victor-Marie Ruprich-Robert ein
Zeuge jener neuen Richtung, die sich innerhalb der École
des Beaux-Arts zur Zeit Sullivans stark bemerkbar
machte, obwohl dieser nicht hier, sondern an der nahen
École des Arts Décoratifs unterrichtete. Doch sein zwischen 1866 und 1876 in verschiedenen Lieferungen her-
ausgegebenes Tafelwerk «Flore ornementale» fand allgemeine Beachtung, und Sullivan kopierte mehrere Blätter
daraus (Abbildung 6 und 7). Diese demonstrieren ein ge-
naues wissenschaftliches Erfassen von Pflanzenformen in
Verbindung mit einer von der Romantischen Schule inspi-
rierten, freien Kompositionsweise.

Sullivans intellektuelle Bindung an die Beaux-Arts läßt
sich zudem an der großen Zahl der Bücher ablesen, die

and 1876, received universal recognition. Drawings of
several leaves which Sullivan copied from this work
(Illustration 6 and 7) demonstrate an exact scientific
understanding of plant forms combined with a free composition inspired by the Romantic School.

Sullivan's intellectual tie to the Beaux-Arts is evident from
the large number of books found in his library on pertinent
subjects. Besides Van Brunt's translation of Viollet-le-
Duc's "Entretiens", he owned several years' issues of the
journals "Revue générale de l'architecture et des travaux
publics", "Encyclopédie d'architecture", and "Croquis
d'architecture" which was published by the students from
the Atelier Questel. Sullivan himself attested to the impact
the Beaux-Arts had on his development in a letter written
to Claude Bragdon on July 25, 1904: "It was certainly in
the school [Ecole des Beaux-Arts], and because of the
teachings of the school, that there entered my mind, fruc-
tified in my mind, the germ of that law which later, after
much observation of nature's processes, I formulated in
the phrase, 'Form follows Function'."

sich in seiner Bibliothek befanden und auf entsprechende Themen bezogen sind. Er besaß neben van Brunts Übersetzung der «Entretiens» von Viollet-le-Duc mehrere Jahrgänge der Zeitschriften «Revue générale de l'architecture et des travaux publics», «Encyclopédie d'architecture» und «Croquis d'architecture», die ein abgerundetes Bild neuerer Tendenzen an der Beaux-Arts ergeben. Es ist aus all dem nur verständlich, wenn Sullivan selbst bezüglich der Beaux-Arts in einem Brief vom 25. Juli 1904 an Claude Bragdon folgende Bilanz zog: «Es war bestimmt an der Schule [die Rede ist von der École des Beaux Arts] und wegen der Lehre an der Schule, daß dort der Keim zu jenem Gesetz sich in meinem Kopf festsetzte und zu entwickeln begann, welches ich später nach vielen Beobachtungen in der Natur im Satz darlegte: Die Form folgt der Funktion.»

Sullivans lebenslangen Kampf gegen Stildiktat und Akademismus kann man durchaus im Einklang mit dem Stoff, den er an der Beaux-Arts vermittelt bekam, betrachten. Mit allgemein gültigen Regeln, die jene der klassischen Ordnungen ablösen sollten, waren etliche Personen beschäftigt, die an der Beaux-Arts lehrten oder ihr nahestanden. Auf ihnen konnte Sullivan aufbauen, seinen eigenen Architekturbegriff entwickeln und schließlich seine Auffassung der Regel ohne Ausnahme («no exception») formulieren.

Adler & Sullivan

Nach Chicago zurückgekehrt arbeitete Sullivan zwischen 1875 und 1880 wahrscheinlich als freier Mitarbeiter für verschiedene Architekten, mit Sicherheit jedoch für Johnston & Edelmann und später für Dankmar Adler. Zum ersten Mal öffentlich erwähnt wurde er 1876 wegen seiner Dekorationen in der Sinai Synagogue und im Moody's Tabernacle, welche mehr Aufsehen erregten als die architektonischen Lösungen. Mit beiden Projekten waren Johnston & Edelmann beauftragt. Da weder die Bauten noch sonst irgendwelche bildlichen Darstellungen überlebt haben, kann nur vermutet werden, daß die Skizzen, die Sullivan von Paris aus an Edelmann geschickt hatte, damit zusammenhängen (siehe S. 49).

Einblicke in Themen, mit denen sich Sullivan in dieser Zeit auseinandersetzte, gewährt ein altes Notizbuch, das er am «Tech» begonnen, aber schon bald wieder aufgegeben hatte. Ab Seite 25 finden sich allerhand Eintragungen über sportliche Leistungen und Muskelumfang verschie-

Sullivan's lifelong battle against academicism and an architecture dictated by style can actually be viewed as consistent with that which he was taught at the Beaux-Arts. At that time, several people closely affiliated with the Beaux-Arts were engaged in establishing a new set of rules to replace those of the classical order. From these rules, Sullivan developed his own "Idea" of architecture, finally formulating his conception of a rule with "no exception".

Adler & Sullivan

Returning to Chicago, Sullivan probably freelanced for various architects between 1875 and 1880, including Johnston & Edelmann and, later, Dankmar Adler. Sullivan was publicly mentioned for the first time in 1876 in conjunction with two commissions of Johnson & Edelmann; his "scandalous" decoration on the Sinai Synagogue and in Moody's Tabernacle had caused more of a sensation than the architectonic solutions themselves. Since neither the buildings nor any illustrations whatsoever have survived, it can only be assumed that the sketches Sullivan sent Edelmann from Paris were designs for those projects (see p. 49).

An old notebook, begun during his stay at "Tech" but discontinued shortly afterwards, provides insights into topics which Sullivan was working on at the time. This notebook is actually an account of the activities of the "Lotos Club", an athletic club with a weekend cabin on the Calumet River. The club's whose founding members included, among others, Sullivan, John Edelmann, and Albert Sullivan, Louis' older brother. The notebook contains numerous entries on various subjects, including results of athletic events and performance, bodily measurements, muscle circumference, sketches of nude models as well as a list of books Sullivan read in 1875. Scattered throughout the book are theoretical and artistic contributions from both Edelmann and Sullivan on architecture and ornament. Edelmann posits that in the future of American art, technical mastery is to be considered subservient to art (p. 27). Sullivan, on the other hand, states: "I believe that the object and aim of distemper decoration is to produce a combination of colors, which shall be harmonious in itself, and with its surroundings; forming a unity, of which the primary function is general effect" (p. 110). In addition, the

8 John Edelmann: Skizzen zum Bates House, Projekt von Burling & Adler («Lotos Club Notebook»).

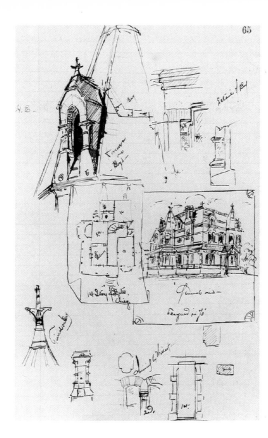

8 John Edelmann: Sketches for Bates House, project by Burling & Adler ("Lotos Club Notebook").

dener Personen, Aktzeichnungen, eine Liste mit Büchern, die Sullivan 1875 gelesen hat. Die meisten stehen im Zusammenhang mit Aktivitäten des «Lotos Club», eines Sportclubs mit Weekendhaus am Calumet River, zu dessen Mitgliedern auch John Edelmann und Albert Sullivan, der ältere Bruder von Louis, zählten. Dazwischen finden sich immer wieder Eintragungen über Architektur und Dekoration, die teils von Edelmann, teils von Sullivan stammen. Edelmann betont etwa, daß in der Zukunft der amerikanischen Kunst die technische Meisterschaft als Diener der Kunst zu betrachten sei (S. 27), während Sullivan weiter hinten formuliert: «Ich glaube, daß der Sinn und Zweck der Dekoration ist, eine Verbindung von Farben zu schaffen, welche in sich und im Kontext harmonisch sein sollte; eine Einheit zu schaffen, deren primärer Zweck der allgemeine Effekt ist.» (S. 110) Die theoretischen Äußerungen werden zudem durch analytische Pflanzenstudien und architektonische Skizzen ergänzt (Abbildung 8). Seinem Ruf entsprechend wurde Sullivan 1880 von Dankmar Adler zunächst mit der Innenausstattung der Central Music Hall betraut. Sullivans Einfluß auf die Entwürfe des

theoretical statements in the notebook are augmented by analytical studies of plants and architectonic sketches (Illustration 8).

In accordance with his reputation as a designer, Dankmar Adler entrusted Sullivan with the task of decorating the interior of the Central Music Hall in 1880. Sullivan's direct influence on the designs increased from project to project. In 1881 Sullivan was promoted to junior partner of "Dankmar Adler & Company". By May 1, 1883, at the age of only twenty-six, Sullivan became a full partner of "Adler & Sullivan", soon to become one of the most important architectural firms of Chicago.

The company received more than 180 commissions from 1880 to 1895. Approximately one third of these were private residences executed primarily for the upper-middle class on the "South Side" of Chicago. Factories and warehouses form the second largest group with 38 commissions (21 %), followed by 33 projects for office buildings (18 %), and 17 designs for theaters or auditoria (9 %). The remaining 31 commissions consist of occa-

Büros vergrößerte sich aber von Projekt zu Projekt. 1881 machte ihn Adler zum Juniorpartner von «Dankmar Adler & Company», und bereits am 1. Mai 1883 stieg er, noch nicht 27jährig, zum gleichberechtigten Partner von «Adler & Sullivan» auf.

Insgesamt erhielt die Firma von 1880 bis 1895 mehr als 180 Aufträge. Rund ein Drittel davon betrafen Wohnbauten, vor allem für die gehobene Mittelschicht auf der «South Side» von Chicago. Fabriken und Lagerhallen machen mit 21 % oder 38 Aufträgen die zweitgrößte Gruppe aus, gefolgt von 33 Projekten für Geschäftshäuser (18 %) und 17 Entwürfen für Theater oder Auditorien (9 %). Die restlichen 31 Aufträge verteilen sich auf vereinzelte Bauaufgaben wie Hotels, Schulen, Eisenbahnstationen, Grabbauten, Kirchen, Bibliotheken, Klubhäuser.

Nicht alle Bauten sind gleich wichtig und verdienen dieselbe Aufmerksamkeit. Adler & Sullivan hielten sich im allgemeinen an die Konventionen der Baugattungen und forcierten ihre Bemühungen um neue konstruktive und gestalterische Lösungen nur dort, wo sie dies aus sozialen und praktischen Gründen für notwendig erachteten. Geschäftshäuser und Auditorien sind Beispiele dafür, wie auf neu eingeführte Bautechniken mit gestalterischen Innovationen reagiert wurde. Grabmäler und teilweise auch Wohnbauten erlaubten gestalterische Freiheiten, während bei den Fabrikbauten immer eine allgemein akzeptierte, reduktionistische Formensprache angewendet wurde. Das Entwurfsverfahren wurde so zumindest anfänglich konsequent den Bedingungen einer Baugattung angepaßt; formale Lösungen für die eine Gattung wurden nicht als Markenzeichen auf andere übertragen. Ausgangspunkt waren vielmehr jeweils die «nackten Tatsachen», von wo aus die ästhetische Gestaltung im Sinne einer physiognomischen Charakterisierung der Aufgabe ihren Anfang nehmen konnte.

In den besten Jahren waren rund 50 Zeichner bei Adler & Sullivan angestellt. Der prominenteste unter ihnen ist zweifellos Frank Lloyd Wright, der von 1888 bis 1893 als «ausführende Hand des Entwurf-Partners» (Wright 1949, S. 53; Abbildung 9) arbeitete und der von Sullivan immer mit größter Achtung als «lieber Meister» gesprochen hat. Die Firma hatte ihren Sitz anfänglich im Borden Block und zog 1889 von dort in die obersten Stockwerke des Turmes des Auditorium Building um.

Die Zusammenarbeit von Adler und Sullivan beruhte auf einer strikten Trennung der Zuständigkeitsbereiche. Adler

sional building projects for hotels, schools, railway stations, tombs, churches, libraries, and clubhouses.

Not all of these buildings are of equal importance or deserve the same amount of consideration. Overall, Adler & Sullivan adhered to the conventions of the various building types, increasing their efforts to find new solutions in construction and design only where deemed necessary for social and practical reasons. Office buildings and auditoria demonstrate how innovations in design were coupled with new industrial capabilities. Tombs, and in part also residences, permitted a greater freedom of expression in design, whereas a more reductive vocabulary of forms was generally used on factory buildings. The design process was, at least initially, consistently adapted to the specific requirements of each building type; the formal solutions for one type were not applied to other types arbitrarily. Rather, the "naked facts" were in each case the point of departure out of which the aesthetic design grew. Thus, the design became in effect a physiognomical characterization of the functional purpose of the specific structural "facts".

At the height of their popularity, there were approximately 50 draftsmen employed at Adler & Sullivan. The most prominent among them was undoubtedly Frank Lloyd Wright. He worked as the "designing partner's pencil" (Wright 3; 1949, p. 53; Illustration 9) from 1888 to 1893 and always spoke of Sullivan with the utmost respect as the "lieber meister". Initially, the firm occupied a suite of offices on the top floor of the Borden Block, the first multi-story office building erected by Dankmar Adler & Co. In 1889, they moved their offices to the top floor of the tower of the Auditorium Building.

The collaboration of Adler and Sullivan was based primarily on a strict separation of their areas of competence; i. e. design and engineering. Adler recognized without reservation "the pre-eminence in the artistic field of Sullivan". Sullivan, on the other hand, entrusted Adler with the technical and the administrative aspects of the business. Nevertheless, Sullivan gradually gained some expertise in this area which would turn out to be very useful to him later.

Adler & Sullivan belong to the heart of the "Chicago School of Architecture". This term denotes neither an actual school, nor an institution, nor does it refer to a common doctrine shared among Chicago architects. In his book "Space, Time, and Architecture" (1941, p. 303),

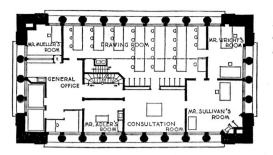

9 Grundriss des Büros von
Adler & Sullivan im Turm des
Auditorium Building, Chicago.

9 Plan of the Adler & Sullivan
office in the Chicago Auditorium.

anerkannte vorbehaltlos «den Vorrang auf künstlerischem Gebiet von Sullivan» (Schuyler 1896, S. 14). Dieser überließ seinerseits Adler den geschäftlichen und technischen Part, allerdings erwarb er sich allmählich auf diesem Gebiet einige Kenntnisse, die ihm später von großem Nutzen sein sollten.

Alder & Sullivan gehören zum harten Kern der «Chicago School of Architecture». Damit ist weder eine wirkliche Schule noch sonst eine Institution oder eine konkret greifbare Doktrin einiger Architekten in Chicago gemeint. Sigfried Giedion leitete den Begriff in «Raum, Zeit, Architektur» (1941, S. 303) von anonymen Bauten ab, die nach dem großen Brand von 1871, erst recht aber nach der wirtschaftlichen Depression von 1873, überall in Chicago aus dem Boden schossen. Diese Bauten waren vorwiegend durch neue technische Mittel geprägt, kaum ornamentiert, getragen von einem feuersicheren Eisenskelett, das große Fensteröffnungen erlaubte. Bereits 1891 hatte sich dafür die Bezeichnung «Chicago Construction» oder «Chicago Commercial Style» etabliert.

Jedoch waren nicht nur anonyme Bauunternehmer an diesem Boom beteiligt. Von den renommierteren Chicagoer Architekturbüros sei insbesondere das von William Le Baron Jenney erwähnt (Abbildung 10). Des weiteren haben auch Peter B. Wight, Solom S. Beman, Burnham & Root, Adler & Sullivan, Holabird & Roche die neuen konstruktiven Möglichkeiten sofort aufgegriffen und begonnen, nach einem entsprechenden formalen Ausdruck zu suchen.

Mit Ausnahme der Einzelfundamente durch Frederick Baumann (1873) und des «Chicago window», eines dreiteiligen Fensters mit beweglichen Seitenflügeln, wurden jedoch alle Erfindungen außerhalb Chicagos gemacht. Es mag deshalb als übertrieben erschienen, von einer «Chicago School» zu sprechen, kommt ihr doch in diesem

Sigfried Giedion derived this term from anonymous buildings which popped up all over Chicago after the Great Fire of 1871, not to mention after the Panic of 1873. The new technical methods had a formative influence on these buildings which were characterized by a lack of ornament and which were supported by a fireproof steel frame clad in bricks which made large window openings possible. By 1891, the term "Chicago Construction" or "Chicago Commercial Style" was already being used to describe buildings with these characteristics.

However, not only anonymous building contractors participated in this construction boom. A number of the more renowned Chicago architectural firms were also involved, in particular that of William Le Baron Jenney (Illustration 10). Furthermore, Peter B. Wight, Solom S. Beman, Burnham & Root, Adler & Sullivan, and Holabird & Roche also took advantage of these new methods of construction and began to search for an appropriate means of formal expression.

With the exception of the isolated pier foundations by Frederick Baumann (1873) and the "Chicago window", a tripartite window with movable side panels, all technical innovations were made outside of Chicago. It may, therefore, seem slightly exaggerated to talk about a "Chicago School", yet it can be credited with being the first to apply these new methods to large-scale projects.

It is, however, important to note that coupled with the willingness with which innovations were introduced in Chicago was an extended and intense debate regarding appropriate forms of expression. Nevertheless, all of those involved in the debate unanimously agreed that the new technical possibilities required a new means of expression. This topic was discussed for many years at various conferences of architect associations as well as in articles published in the "Inland Architect", Chicago's leading architectural journal. Interestingly enough, sev-

Sinne höchstens das Verdienst zu, neue Methoden im großen Umfang angewandt zu haben.

Doch ist zusätzlich in Betracht zu ziehen, daß mit der Bereitwilligkeit, mit der das Neue in Chicago eingeführt wurde, eine längere und intensiv geführte Debatte über adäquate Ausdrucksformen verbunden war. Einhellig gingen alle Beteiligten davon aus, daß die neuen technischen Möglichkeiten auch eine neue Ausdrucksweise notwendig machen. Das Thema wurde über Jahre hinweg auf Tagungen verschiedener Architekturvereinigungen oder auch im «Inland Architect», Chicagos wichtigster Architekturzeitschrift, behandelt. Bezeichnenderweise hatten einige größere Büros einen «designing partner» (Root, Roche, Sullivan), der speziell für Fragen der Gestaltung zuständig war. Dies als Hinweis dafür, daß sich die Büros nicht zuletzt auch auf dem Gebiet Gestaltung zu übertrumpfen suchten. Sullivan akzeptierte insbesondere den 1891 verstorbenen John Root, den «designing partner» von Daniel Burnham, als ebenbürtigen Rivalen.

Die Rivalität zwischen Root und Sullivan zeigt sich beispielhaft in einem Vergleich zwischen dem Rookery Building (Burnham & Root, 1886–1887; Abbildung 11) und dem Auditorium Building (Adler & Sullivan, 1886–1889; Abbildung 12) zum Ausdruck. Beide Bauten entstanden

eral of the larger firms had a "designing partner" (Root, Roche, Sullivan), who was specifically in charge of questions regarding design. This also indicates that the firms had a keen interest in outdoing themselves in this area. In particular, Sullivan regarded John Root, Daniel Burnham's "designing partner", who died prematurely in 1891, as an equal rival.

The rivalry between Root and Sullivan is evident in a comparison between the Rookery Building (Burnham & Root, 1886–87, Illustration 11), and the Auditorium Building (Adler & Sullivan, 1886–89, Illustration 12). The design of both buildings was directly influenced by the warehouse built in the Romanesque style by Henry Hobson Richardson for Marshall Field in Chicago (1885–87, Illustration 13). Differences are apparent, however, in that Root used a vocabulary of Romanesque forms that diverged slightly from Richardson's, whereas Sullivan only utilized the abstract composition scheme of the façade.

Root sheds light on his position in an essay published in the "Inland Architect" in 1885. Here, he emphasizes that decoration should only play a subordinate role in design: "It (the decoration) must follow the form in which they best do their work" (Root 1885, p. 89). Sullivan, on the other hand, always spoke out against any kind of subor-

11 Burnham & Root: Rookery
Building, Chicago, 1886–87.

11 *Burnham & Root: Rookery
Building, Chicago, 1886–87.*

12 Adler & Sulllivan:
Auditorium Building, Chicago,
1886–89.

12 *Adler & Sullivan:
Auditorium Building, Chicago,
1886–89.*

13 Henry H. Richardson:
Warenhaus, Marshall Fields,
Chicago, 1885–87.

13 *Henry H. Richardson:
Marshall Fields Department
Store, Chicago, 1885–87.*

unter dem Eindruck des von Henry H. Richardson im romanesken Stil erbauten Warenhauses für Marshall Fields in Chicago (1885–1887; Abbildung 13). Unterschiede zeigen sich vor allem insofern, als Root ein von Richardson verschiedenes Vokabular romanischer Formen benützte, während Sullivan überhaupt nur das abstrakte Kompositionsschema der Fassaden übernahm.

Roots Position wird verständlich durch seinen Essay im «Inland Architect» aus dem Jahre 1885. Hier betont er, daß die Dekoration eine bloß untergeordnete Rolle spiele: «Sie [die Dekoration] muß der Form folgen, in der sie ihre Aufgabe am besten erfüllen kann» (Root 1885, S. 89). Sullivan dagegen sprach sich immer gegen jede Unterordnung des Ornaments aus, indem er sogar die Problemstellung an sich kritisierte. Niemand würde ihm zufolge ernsthaft fragen, was an einem Baum wesentlicher ist, Ast oder Blatt (Sullivan 1887, S. 31). Wer vermöchte also zu sagen, was an einem Bauwerk wesentlicher ist, Konstruktion oder Dekoration.[1] Während Root das Konzept einer «dekorierten Konstruktion» vorläufig akzeptierte, erfand Sullivan eine Metapher, die die vermeintlichen Gegensätze in einer völlig neuen Konstellation zueinander erkennen ließ. Root war bereit, sich der historischen Stilformen behelfsmäßig – bis zur Erfindung eines amerikanischen Stils – zu bedienen, doch Sullivan hatte eine neuartige Vermittlung zwischen Ornament und Eisenkonstruktion im Sinne, die er als gleichermaßen konstituierend für die Architektur betrachtete.

Von einer «Chicago School of Architecture» kann demzufolge mit um so größerer Berechtigung gesprochen werden, wenn neben der Konstruktion auch die formalen Komponenten berücksichtigt werden. Konstruktion hat nicht den Stellenwert eines absoluten Maßstabs der Architektur, sondern eher eine Art von Versuchsanordnung, die zur Entwicklung neuer architektonischer Beziehungen zwischen Struktur und Fassade, zwischen innen und außen dient. Nur so gesehen war die «Chicago School of Architecture» wirklich innovativ und Adler & Sullivan ihre wichtigsten Vertreter.

Auditorien

Die Projekte für Auditorien verschiedenster Art (Theater, Konzertsäle, Kirchenräume) machen zwar nur etwa ein Zehntel des gesamten Auftragsbestandes von Adler & Sullivan aus, erreichen jedoch umsatzmäßig mehr als die

dination of ornament, criticizing even the way the problem itself was approached. While Root had accepted the concept of a "decorated structure", Sullivan used a metaphor that revealed the seeming opposites in a completely new relationship to each other. According to him, no one would ever seriously ask which is more essential on a tree, branch or leaf (Sullivan 1887, p. 31). Who then would be capable of saying, which is more essential on a building, structure or decoration?[1] Root was willing to make use of historical styles if necessary – until an American style of its own was invented. Sullivan, on the other hand, proposed a new type of interdependence between ornament and steel-frame construction which he viewed as equally essential for architecture.

One can, therefore, speak of a "Chicago School of Architecture" with much greater legitimacy if the formal components are considered along with the new type of construction. Structure does not have the status of an absolute standard of architecture but, rather, acts as a kind of working model for ordering the architectonic elements for the purpose of developing a new relationship between structure and façade, between inside and outside. Thus, the "Chicago School of Architecture" was from this perspective truly innovative and Adler & Sullivan its most important representatives.

Auditoria

The projects for various types of auditoria (theaters, concert halls, churches) constitute only about one tenth of the total number of commissions of Adler & Sullivan, yet they represent more than half of the total sum of money used by the firm for building. Auditoria were Adler's first large commissions and they were also the first buildings which Adler & Sullivan erected outside of Chicago. That Adler was engaged as a consultant during the construction of Carnegie Hall in New York 1889 is evidence of the growing national recognition of the firm. The eleven theater projects that were built or remodelled, eight of them in Chicago, comprise the most important commissions in this group. The only theater still standing is the Auditorium Building, the most expensive project that Adler & Sullivan ever built: With a budget of over 3 million dollars, it cost as much as approximately 25 private residences or six Wainwright Buildings.

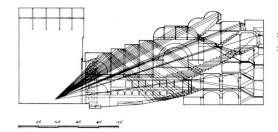

14 Chicago Auditorium, schematischer Längsschnitt.

14 Chicago Auditorium, schematic longitudinal section.

Hälfte der Summe, die durch die Firma verbaut worden ist. Durch Auditorien kam Adler zu seinen ersten größeren Aufträgen, und Auditorien waren auch die ersten Bauten, die Adler & Sullivan außerhalb Chicagos errichten konnten. Es deutet auch auf die wachsende nationale Anerkennung der Firma hin, wenn Adler 1889 beim Bau der Carnegie Hall in New York als Berater beigezogen wurde. Insbesondere fallen die elf Theaterbauten respektive -umbauten ins Gewicht, von denen acht allein in Chicago realisiert wurden. Davon ist einzig das Auditorium Building erhalten geblieben. Es stellt das teuerste Projekt dar, das Adler & Sullivan jemals gebaut haben: Mit über drei Millionen Dollar kostete es soviel wie etwa 25 Einfamilienhäuser oder 6 Wainwright-Hochhäuser.

Die Theaterbauten können Aufschluß darüber geben, wie die Zusammenarbeit zwischen Adler und Sullivan konkret funktionierte. Obwohl Sullivans Anteil in zeitgenössischen Berichten jeweils größeres Echo fand, bleibt unbestritten, daß er mit seinen Dekorationen auf technische und strukturelle Neuerungen reagierte, die von Adler eingebracht wurden. Diese Sachverhalte aber waren es in erster Linie, die die jeweiligen Bauherren bewogen, den Auftrag an Adler & Sullivan zu vergeben. Adlers herausragende Pionierleistung in diesem Zusammenhang bestand darin, die wissenschaftlichen Untersuchungen des schottischen Ingenieurs John Scott Russell (1808–1882) über die Ausbreitung von Schallwellen im Raum in einem vollkommen neuen Typus von Theatersaal umgesetzt zu haben (Abbildung 14).

Die typischen Merkmale des traditionellen Saals faßte Adler selbst wie folgt zusammen: Zentralraum mit Kuppel überhöht und mit ebenem Fußboden, umgeben von Wänden, die mit Balkonen besetzt sind. Je größer nun das Fassungsvermögen der Säle sein sollte, um so schwieriger wurde es, innerhalb des alten Systems für alle Plätze gute optische und akustische Verhältnisse zu schaffen. Für das Chicagoer Opern-Festival (1885) beispielsweise mußten

By examining the theater buildings more closely, we can find out how the collaboration between Adler and Sullivan actually worked. Although Sullivan's contribution usually met with the most enthusiastic response in contemporary articles, it remains undisputed that his decoration was a reaction to the technical and structural innovations which were introduced by Adler. These facts played a major role in convincing prospective clients to award a commission to Adler & Sullivan. Adler's outstanding pioneer achievement in the field of acoustics consisted in having transformed the scientific observations of the Scottish engineer John Scott Russell (1808–82) regarding the movement of sound waves in space into a completely new type of auditorium (Illustration 14).

Adler himself summarized the typical features of a traditional auditorium as follows: a central space surmounted by a cupola with a level floor surrounded by walls that support balconies. The greater the seating capacity of the theater, the more difficult it was within the old system to create good visual and acoustic conditions for every seat. For the Chicago Opera Festival (1885), for instance, Adler & Sullivan had to design an auditorium which could hold 6200 people at one time; not to mention the 4237 regular seats calculated for the Auditorium Building (1886–89).

Adler's most important innovations with respect to the auditorium were numerous: reduction of the volume of space by employing a funnel-shaped design that becomes increasingly narrow toward the stage; a gradual rise of the main floor calculated on the basis of Scott Russell's "isacoustic curve" and adapted to the specific architectonic requirements; uneven surfaces which were to absorb sound near the stage and diminish reverberation; the rear section, on the other hand, was smooth to reflect sound since reverberation was desirable as long as it reached the auditor within approximately one-tenth of a second after the direct outward movement of sound

Adler & Sullivan einen Saal schaffen, in dem 6200 Personen einer Aufführung beiwohnen konnten; beim Auditorium Building (1886–89) wurde immerhin mit 4237 regulären Plätzen gerechnet.

Adlers wichtigste Neuerungen in bezug auf den Zuschauerraum waren: Minimalisierung des Raumvolumens, das sich gegen die Bühne hin trichterförmig verkleinerte; Ansteigen der Zuschauerränge; gebrochene Oberflächen, die im bühnennahen Bereich schallschluckend sein sollten, um Widerhall zu verhindern, im hinteren Teil dagegen glatt, da hier Widerhall erwünscht war, sofern er innerhalb von etwa einer Zehntelsekunde nach dem direkten Schallimpuls beim Hörer auftraf; und schließlich die rückwärtige Öffnung des Zuschauerraums, um jede unkontrollierte Reflexion von Schallwellen an der Rückwand zu vermeiden. Zudem war sich Adler bewußt, daß die akustischen Bedingungen bei einer Orchesteraufführung andere sein würden als beim Sprechtheater. Deswegen hat er bei diesen eine maximale Größe von 2500 Plätzen eingehalten. Beim Auditorium Building von Chicago dagegen, wo beide Optionen offengehalten werden sollten, konnten die beiden obersten Galerien mit herunterklappbaren Deckenelementen geschlossen und das Raumvolumen auf diese Art reduziert werden.

Die unförmige Gestalt des Raumes und seine schiere Größe gaben Sullivan jeweils schwierige Bedingungen für die Gestaltung vor. Auch wenn er mit den dekorativen Elementen keine tektonische Ordnung im nachhinein vortäuschte, so war das System der Ausstattung doch nicht beliebig. Die Lösung bestand darin, jede Wandfläche, jedes Gewölbe und jeden Bogen mit Ornamenten zu versehen und gegenüber benachbarten Teilen durch Rahmen abzugrenzen. Diese große Anzahl raumbegrenzender Elemente – «ein Nebeneinander von herabstoßenden Kurven und ebenso deren gegenläufige Pendants», wie Robert Venturi bezüglich des Auditoriums schrieb (1966, S. 91) – wurde aber andererseits durch die Abstimmung der Farbtöne und durch den Sog der Bühne in einen auch räumlich einheitlichen Klangkörper verwandelt. Von den hintersten Reihen stürzt der Blick hinunter in die Tiefe, geleitet von glitzernden Schalen, die sich immer enger werdend trichterförmig um die Bühnenöffnung legen.

Diese Gestaltungsweise übertrug Sullivan später vom Innenraum auf Fassaden (Jordy 1986, S. 135). Das Stufenportal des Transportation Building (1891–93) an der Weltausstellung von Chicago kann als nach außen gestülpter Bühnentrichter interpretiert werden, die Fassa-

waves; and finally, the main floor was open toward the back in order to prevent any uncontrolled reflection of the sound waves on the rear wall. In addition, Adler was keenly aware that the acoustic conditions for an orchestral performance were different from those of a stage performance. For this reason, Adler restricted the size of a stage theater to a maximum of 2500 seats. However, since the Auditorium Building in Chicago was to be used for both purposes, the total volume of the room could be decreased by closing off both of the upper galleries with mobile ceiling elements, thereby greatly reducing the seating capacity of the theater.

The cumbersome shape of the room as well as its sheer size made designing this space difficult from the start. Even if Sullivan did not intend to suggest a tectonic order with the decorative elements, the system of interior decoration was far from arbitrary. His solution consisted in covering each wall surface, each vault, and each arch with ornament, using frames to define them spatially from adjacent elements. Through the unifying effect of the coordinated shades of color as well as the funnel-shaped opening of the stage, Sullivan was able to harmonize this vast number of discordant elements – "juxtapositions of swooping curves and diverse repetitions" (Venturi 1966, p. 64) as Robert Venturi wrote in reference to the Auditorium Building – into a visually uniform space. Looking down from the last row of seats, the eye is pulled toward the stage guided by the funnel-shaped gilded ceiling panels glittering with hundreds of electric lights.

Sullivan later transferred this design scheme from interiors to exteriors (Jordy 186, p. 135). For instance, the stepped portal of the Transportation Building (1891–93) at the World Exposition in Chicago can be interpreted as a "stage funnel" turned inside out; or the decorative treatment of the terra-cotta sheathing, a non-self-supporting exterior casing on the Guaranty Building in Buffalo (1895–96), becomes the dominant theme of the whole façade.

Office Buildings

The office buildings of Adler & Sullivan deserve mention for two reasons in particular. First, they belong to those buildings which epitomize the "Chicago School of Architecture". Secondly, the struggle to find formal solu-

15 Ed. Guillaume: Maison commerciale, Paris («Revue générale d'architecture», 1880).

15 Ed. Guillaume: Maison commerciale, Paris ("Revue générale d'architecture" 1880).

den des Guaranty Building in Buffalo (1895–96) haben die dekorative Behandlung der nicht-tragenden Verkleidung zum Thema.

Geschäftshäuser

Die Geschäftshäuser der Firma Adler & Sullivan verdienen aus zwei Gründen speziell erwähnt zu werden. Erstens gehören sie zu jenen Bauten, die den Inbegriff der «Chicago School of Architecture» ausmachen. Zweitens ist hier am deutlichsten das Ringen um formale Lösungen, die den technischen Neuerungen entsprechen, erkennbar. Die Geschäftshäuser von Adler & Sullivan lassen sich chronologisch ebenso wie formal in drei Gruppen einteilen: die neu-griechischen, die richardsonesken und die Wolkenkratzer.

Die erste Gruppe entstand ausnahmslos im Zentrum von Chicago. Bereits beim Borden Block (1880) läßt sich die neue Handschrift Sullivans ausmachen. Während Adler zuvor die übereinanderliegenden Geschosse, wie es in Chicago üblich war, jeweils horizontal betonte, wurden sie durch Sullivan vertikal zusammengefaßt. In der Regel unterschied er bloß noch zwischen drei Zonen, die der

tions truly appropriate for the technical innovations is clearly evident here. The office buildings of Adler & Sullivan can be chronologically as well as formally divided into three categories: Néo-grec, the Richardsonesque and the skyscrapers.

The first group of Néo-grec office buildings was erected entirely in the downtown center of Chicago. Sullivan's signature is already evident on the first multi-story office building of Adler and Sullivan, the Borden Block (1880). While Adler previously emphasized the horizontality of the floors, as was usual in Chicago, Sullivan unified the floors vertically. Normally, he made only a distinction between three zones, subdividing the façade like a columnar shaft to correspond to the tripartite division of classical architecture: base, shaft, and attic. The shaft extending over several floors consists alternatively of surfaces of masonry and of glass with cast-iron frames. This vertical unification of the floors and the overall composition of the façade echoes fashionable trends in Paris at the time (Illustration 15). The ornament, removed from the structural elements and integrated into large non-supporting surfaces, consists of palmettes and lotus blossoms often carved into the stone like bas reliefs. Sullivan's proclivity for Egyptian and Byzantine decorative forms, which were

klassischen Dreiteilung entsprechen: Sockel, Schaft und Dachgeschoß. Der Schaft wiederum besteht aus gemauerten Teilen und Binnenflächen aus Glas und Gußeisenrahmen, die über mehrere Stockwerke reichen. Für dieses Zusammenfassen der Geschosse lassen sich damals aktuelle Beispiele aus Paris zum Vergleich heranziehen (Abbildung 15). Die Ornamente wurden von den strukturellen Teilen abgezogen und in ausfachende Flächen integriert. Sie stellen geometrisierte Palmetten und Lotusblüten dar, die oft als Reliefs in den Stein eingelassen wurden. Auch dies entspricht formalen Vorlieben der Romantischen Schule in Paris für ägyptisierende und byzantinische Schmuckformen, wie sie etwa Ruprich-Robert in «Flore ornementale» darstellte.

Die zweite Gruppe von Geschäftshäusern entstand unmittelbar nach dem Bau des Auditorium Building (1886–89) und ist wie dieses inspiriert von der Architektur Richardsons, insbesondere natürlich dessen Marshall Fields Warenhaus (1885–87) in Chicago. Wie bereits das Auditorium Building in bezeichnender Weise von diesem Vorbild abwich, so auch das Walker Warehouse (1888–89) und der Dooly Block (1890–91). Da die Fassaden aus glatt geschliffenen Quadersteinen erbaut wurden und da die großen Rundbogen mit mehrstufig abgetreppten Laibungen versehen waren, ist man verführt, wiederum an Pariser Beispiele zu denken, etwa an das Gebäude von Vaudremer an der Rue de la Monnaie. Im Vergleich zur ersten Gruppe hatte Sullivan die architektonischen Elemente und Schmuckformen vereinfacht. Die Bauvolumen wirken wie homogene Blöcke, in welche Öffnungen scharf eingeschnitten sind. Bloß die Portiken heben sich jeweils davon ab, wie vor die Fassadenflucht gestellte Scheiben.

Die dritte Gruppe schließlich umfaßt die eigentlichen Hochhäuser, angeführt vom Wainwright Building (1890–92), gefolgt vom Projekt für den Fraternity Temple (1891), dem Union Trust Building (1892–93) und dem Guaranty Building (1894–96). Bevor solche Bauten mit 9, 12 und mehr Geschossen überhaupt möglich und sicher genug waren, mußte dafür gesorgt werden, daß die Außenwände trotz zunehmender Bauhöhe relativ dünn blieben und mit großen Öffnungen versehen werden konnten. Die Lösung bestand in einem Skelett aus Bessemerstahl, an welches die Fassaden bloß angehängt wurden. Zum ersten Mal sind diese Voraussetzungen 1884 von William Le Baron Jenney beim Home Insurance Building in Chicago für ein mehrgeschossiges Geschäftshaus

illustrated in Ruprich-Robert's "Flore ornementale", also recalls forms preferred by the Romantic School.

Erected immediately after the construction of the Auditorium Building (1886–89), the second group of office buildings was, like the Auditorium, inspired by the architecture of Richardson, particularly his Marshall Field Wholesale Store (1885–87) in Chicago. Just as the Auditorium Building already diverged from its model in a distinctive way, so did the Walker Warehouse (1888–89) and the Dooly Block (1890–91). The façades constructed of smoothly polished ashlar masonry with large round arches articulated by reveals recessed in steps from the wall plane recall similar examples in Paris, such as Vaudremer's building in the Rue de la Monnaie. In contrast to the first group of Néo-grec office buildings, the Richardsonesque buildings are characterized by a simplification of the architectonic elements and decorative forms. In most cases, the building mass consists of an homogeneous cube with clean-cut openings stamped into the façade. Only the porticos project slightly, like panels placed in front of the wall plane.

The third group consists of the actual skyscrapers, beginning with the Wainwright Building (1890–92), followed by the project for the Fraternity Temple (1891), then the Union Trust Building (1892–93), and finally the Guaranty Building (1894–96). Before buildings of nine or more stories were possible and safe, the architects had to make sure that the exterior walls, despite the increased building height, remained relatively thin, thus permitting larger openings to bring more natural light to the interior. The solution consisted in constructing a frame of bessemer steel to which the façades were simply attached. These requirements for a tall multi-story office building were first met in 1884 with William Le Baron Jenney's Home Insurance Building in Chicago (Illustration 16). This new method of steel-frame construction was later utilized in a very impressive way by Holabird and Roche in the Tacoma Building (1887–89, Illustration 17), and by Burnham & Co. in the Reliance Building (1891–94, Illustration 18). When compared to the last two buildings in particular, the skyscrapers of Adler & Sullivan seem awkward and heavy and do not necessarily suggest the slender steel frame underneath the exterior casing. Despite this new type of construction, their buildings are still characterized by a blockiness typical of Richardson which is emphasized by the classical tripartite division of the building mass (base, shaft, capital). At the same time, there is noticeably

16 William Le Baron Jenney:
Home Insurance Building,
Chicago, 1884.

16 William Le Baron Jenney:
Home Insurance Building,
Chicago, 1884.

17 Holabird & Roche: Tacoma Building, Chicago, 1887–89.
17 Holabird & Roche: Tacoma Building, Chicago, 1887–89.

18 Burnham & Co.: Reliance Building, Chicago, 1891–94.
18 Burnham & Co.: Reliance Building, Chicago, 1891–94.

erfüllt worden (Abbildung 16). Das neue strukturelle Prinzip wurde in der Folge auf sehr eindrückliche Weise von Holabird & Roche im Tacoma Building (1887–89, Abbildung 17) zum Ausdruck gebracht oder von Burnham & Co. beim Reliance Building (1891–94; Abbildung 18). Verglichen vor allem mit den beiden letzteren wirken die Hochhäuser von Adler & Sullivan schwerfällig und lassen hinter der Verkleidung nicht zwingenderweise ein schlankes Eisenskelett vermuten. Trotz neuer konstruktiver Struktur zeichnen sie sich nach wie vor durch eine an Richardson erinnernde Blockhaftigkeit aus, unterstützt durch eine klassische Dreiteilung der Volumen (Sockel, Schaft und Kapitell). Gleichzeitig ist eine Zunahme der Dekorationen zu beobachten, die beim Guaranty Building im «all-over» der fein reliefierten Tonplatten gipfelt. Aus der tektonisch aufgebauten Wand ist eine dekorativ vorgehängte Hülle geworden, deren Gestalt gänzlich durch die Öffnungen und die Art, wie diese durch dekorierte (Bilder-)Rahmen zusammengefaßt werden, bestimmt ist.

Sullivans Bemühungen um eine gestalterische Lösung für das Hochhaus fanden ihre Zusammenfassung in zwei Essays: «Ornament in Architecture» (1892) und «The Tall Office Building Artistically Considered» (1896). In beiden Texten beginnt Sullivan mit der Behauptung, daß die elementare und logische Form eines Gebäudes, so dürftig sie auch aussehen möge, für die künftige Entwicklung der Architektur zwar von Interesse sei, doch mitnichten ersetze sie die künstlerische Form. Der architektonische Ausdruck beginne da, wo es um die individuelle Einheit einer Aufgabe gehe. Damit diese Einheit eine «wirkliche und poetische Einheit» darstelle, sollte «das Ornament nicht als etwas erscheinen [...], das den Geist der Struktur aufnimmt, sondern als etwas, das diesen Geist vermöge seines andersgearteten Wachstums ausdrückt» (Sullivan 1892, S. 83). Und auch: Struktur und Ornament würden so zusammengehören, wie ein bestimmtes Blatt zu einem bestimmten Baum gehöre.

Während Sullivan zunächst von einer Sympathie zwischen Ornament und Konstruktion schreibt, die sich gegenseitig steigern und zu einer individuellen Einheit der Gestalt führen sollen, ersetzt er diesen Gedanken im zweiten Text durch seine berühmte Formel «form ever follows function». Der unmittelbare Zusammenhang ist folgender: «Ob wir an den im Flug gleitenden Adler, die geöffnete Apfelblüte, das schwer sich abmühende Zugpferd, den

more ornament used, reaching its culmination in the finely carved terra-cotta tiles "all-over" every exposed surface of the Guaranty Building. In this case, Sullivan has replaced a tectonically structured wall by a decorative curtain-like skin whose design is determined by the disposition of the openings and the way decorated (picture) frames are used to connect them.

Sullivan's efforts to find a formal solution appropriate for the tall building were summarized in two essays: "Ornament in Architecture" (1892), and "The Tall Office Building Artistically Considered" (1896). Sullivan begins both texts with the claim that although the basic and logical form of a building, however bare it may look, is of interest for the future development of architecture, it can, however, never replace the artistic form. Architectonic expression begins where the unity of form and function is realized in a unique and individual way. In order for this unity to constitute a "real and poetic unity", "the ornament should appear, not as something receiving the spirit of the structure, but as a thing expressing that spirit by virtue of differential growth" (Sullivan 1892, p. 83). Furthermore, it follows that a particular kind of ornament belongs to a particular kind of structure, just as a certain kind of leaf belongs to a certain kind of tree.

Sullivan writes initially about a "sympathy" between ornament and structure in which these two elements evolve together toward a unified and individual design concept by reciprocally intensifiying each other. He replaces this idea in the second essay with his famous formula "form ever follows function". The exact context is as follows: "Whether it be the sweeping eagle in his flight or the open apple-blossom, the toiling work-horse, the blithe swan, the branching oak, the winding stream at its base, the drifting clouds, over all the coursing sun, form ever follows function, and this is the law" (Sullivan, 1896, p. 111).

Usually this axiom is interpreted to affirm that the form of a building can be derived directly from its functional requirements. Sullivan's arguments point, however, to another concept of function that includes both physical and symbolic elements. His concept is closely related to the theories of Johann Caspar Lavater who attempted to explain the variety of human expression scientifically. For instance, in a chapter entitled "About the Study of Physiognomy" Lavater writes: "Nature forms man according to one standard; which, however various, always continues, like the pantograph, in the same parallelism and

majestätischen Schwan, die weit ihre Äste breitende Eiche, den Grund des sich windenden Stroms, die ziehenden Wolken oder die über allem strahlende Sonne denken: immer folgt die Form der Funktion – und das ist das Gesetz.» (Sullivan 1896, S. 111)

Üblicherweise wird diese Formel so gedeutet, als sollte eine Gebäudeform direkt aus funktionellen Bedingungen abgeleitet werden können. Die Argumentationsweise Sullivans ebenso wie die von ihm angeführten Beispiele deuten jedoch auf einen andern Funktionsbegriff hin, der physische und symbolische Momente einschließt. Sullivans Bemühen gleicht dabei jenem von Johann Caspar Lavater, der die Vielfalt des menschlichen Ausdrucks wissenschaftlich zu erklären versuchte. Lavater schreibt etwa im Kapitel «Über das Studium der Physiognomik»: «Die Natur bildet alle Menschen nach *einer* Grundform, welche nur auf unendlich mannigfaltige Weise verschoben wird, immer aber im Parallelismus und denselben Proportionen bleibt, wie der Pantagraph oder das Parallellineal.» (Lavater 1778, 4. Bd., S. 459) Entsprechend wollte Sullivan aufgrund eines einzigen Gesetzes die Vielfalt im architektonischen Ausdruck («wie beim Menschen») begründen. Mit dieser physiognomischen Interpretation von «form follows function» läßt sich eine Brücke herstellen zwischen dem Entwurfsverfahren und den physiognomischen Metaphern, auf die Sullivan bei der Beschreibung von Bauten auffällig häufig zurückgriff.[2]

Angewandt auf Sullivans Hochhaus-Trilogie (Wainwright-, Guaranty- und Bayard Building), die im gleichen Zeitraum wie die beiden oben zitierten Texte entstand, läßt sich sagen: Obschon die Eisenkonstruktion nicht sichtbar gemacht, sondern sogar über das notwendige Maß hinaus verdeckt wird, ist sie gleichwohl an der Fassade manifest. Denn sie ist die Voraussetzung dafür, daß die Fassade ihre konventionelle Rolle radikal verändern konnte; sie ist nunmehr ohne tragende Funktion, entlassen folglich auch aus der Pflicht, den tektonischen Aufbau auszudrücken. Gottfried Sempers Vorstellung der Wand als einer ursprünglich textilen Abtrennung mit «‹all-over› treatment» (Semper 1860, S. 42), wird in dieser Hinsicht wieder aktuell (vergleiche dazu Frampton in: Weingarden 1987, S. IX).

Konstrukteur und Dekorateur arbeiten nach je eigenen Gesetzen. Programmatisch hatte dies Sullivan zuerst beim Transportation Building (Entwurf 1891) durchgespielt und später beim Guaranty Building (1894–96) in Buffalo, dessen Dekorationen wie tätowiert aussehen oder aber

proportion" (Lavater 1778, vol. 2, p. 50). Correspondingly, Sullivan attempted to explain the variety in architectonic expression ("as with people") using one single principle. This physiognomical interpretation of "form follows function" spans the gap between the process of design and the striking physiological metaphors Sullivan frequently used when describing buildings.[2]

When applied to Sullivan's tall building trilogy (Wainwright Building, Guaranty Building, Bayard Building), erected about the same time as both the texts cited above were written, one can say that although the steel-frame construction is not made visible but, rather, concealed to a greater degree than necessary, it is nonetheless manifest on the façade. For it was precisely because of this steel-frame construction that the façade could radically transform its conventional role: since the façade no longer has a load-bearing function, it is consequently released from the task of expressing the tectonic structure of a wall. In this respect, Gottfried Semper's idea of the wall as originally a textile divider with "'all-over' treatment" (Semper 1860, p. 42) is relevant again (cf. Frampton in Weingarden 1987, p. IX).

Engineer and designer now work according to their own laws. Sullivan first experimented programmatically with this idea on the Transportation Building (design, 1891), then again on the Guaranty Building (1894–96) in Buffalo. Here, the decoration appears almost as if tatooed onto the wall surface, recalling an Ancient Egyptian temple, in which every surface is covered with hieroglyphics (Illustrations 19 and 20). In the freedom that resulted from contact with the new structural system, Sullivan launched his famous dictum "form follows function". In other words, he did not attempt to formulate a law in opposition to the autonomy of structure and ornament; rather, he formulated a law wherein the various architectonic systems could refer to and influence each other.

It is, thus, not coincidental that a breakthrough in decoration coincided with the breakthrough of the steel frame. This type of construction made it possible to design an exterior as a physiognomical expression of the interior. Sullivan's "all-over" decorative treatment of the façade is, on closer analysis, actually an interweaving of several decorative frames which, on the one hand, emphasize the contours of the building and, on the other, surround and unite the openings into groups that are characteristic of their function. Thus, the openings, transitions between inside and outside, function like the eyes of a human

19 Ruinen von Karnak
(Zeichnung aus «Croquis
d'architecture», 1867).

19 Carnac ruins (drawing
from "Croquis d'archi-
tecture", 1867).

20 Adler & Sullivan:
Guaranty Building, Buffalo,
1894–96.

20 Adler & Sullivan:
Guaranty Building, Buffalo,
1894–96.

an die altägyptische Art der Beschriftung von Säulen und Wänden denken lassen, zu einer extremen Vollendung gebracht (Abbildung 19 und 20). In den Freiraum aber, der sich solchermaßen aus dem Umgang mit dem neuen strukturellen System eröffnete, warf Sullivan sein «form follows function». Damit ist gemeint, daß er nicht gegen, sondern aufgrund der Autonomie von Konstruktion und Dekoration ein Gesetz zu formulieren versuchte, wonach die verschiedenen architektonischen Systeme aufeinander Bezug nehmen können.

countenance which, when viewed from the outside, act as "windows to the soul".

The "sympathy" between such unequal things as structure and ornament, between inside and outside, the superficial and the essential, could be interpreted as "weak architecture", a concept that Ignazio Solà-Morales borrowed from the philosopher Gianni Vattimo. The decoration on Sullivan's buildings brings thus the fundamentally decorative character of all architecture into focus. Robert Venturi's notion of the "decorated shed" is

Es ist also nicht zufällig, daß mit dem Durchbruch des Eisenskeletts ein Durchbruch in der Ornamentierung festzustellen ist. Das Eisenskelett stellt die Bedingung der Möglichkeit dar, Fassaden als physiognomischen Ausdruck des Innern zu gestalten. Die «all-over»-Behandlung bei Sullivan läßt sich als Verschränkung mehrerer dekorativer Rahmen lesen, die einerseits die Umrisse des Bauvolumens betonen und andererseits die Öffnungen auf charakteristische Weise umgeben und zusammenfassen. Die Übergänge zwischen Innen und Außen erhalten insofern die Bedeutung von Augen im menschlichen Antlitz, welche von außen gesehen als Spiegel des Innern gelten.

Die Sympathie zwischen so ungleichen Dingen wie Ornament und Konstruktion, zwischen Außen und Innen, Oberflächlichem und Wesentlichem könnte im Sinne einer «schwachen Architektur» interpretiert werden, um hier den Begriff von Ignazio Solà-Morales zu gebrauchen, den dieser in Anlehnung an den Turiner Philosophen Gianni Vattimo benutzt. Das Dekorative in den Bauten Sullivans erweist sich so als das Ins-Zentrum-Rücken des grundlegend dekorativen Charakters aller Architektur. Als weitere «postmoderne» Erklärung bietet sich auch Robert Venturis Konzept des «decorated shed» an. Sullivans Bauten sind solchen postmodernen Aufmerksamkeiten deshalb zugänglich, weil hier die Spannungen und Brüche zwischen verschiedenen architektonischen Mitteln nicht außer acht gelassen werden. Was sie von den postmodernen Enkeln und Urenkeln andererseits unterscheidet, ist, daß Sullivan letztlich an eine Versöhnung der verschiedenen Systeme «mit je andersgeartetem Wachstum» glaubte.

Höhepunkt und Fall

1892 verzeichneten Adler & Sullivan, bedingt durch die allgemeine wirtschaftliche Konjunktur, einen Rückgang im Auftragsbestand um etwa 50 %. Dieser Trend hielt an, auch nachdem sich die allgemeine Lage wieder zu erholen begann. Der einzige Auftrag im Jahre 1895 war jener für das Guaranty Building in Buffalo. Sullivan glaubte, für den schlechten Geschäftsgang die Chicagoer Weltausstellung von 1893 verantwortlich machen zu können, weil durch sie ein Geschmacksvirus ausgesetzt worden sei, der sich im Mittleren Westen zunächst eine Zeitlang still eingenistet habe, bis er plötzlich in einem eklektischen Fieber ausgebrochen sei (Sullivan 1922/23, S. 322).

Daß Adler sich im Juli 1895 vom Geschäft zurückzog,

another "postmodern" concept which applies here. Sullivan's buildings lend themselves to such ideas precisely because the tensions and gaps between various architectonic systems are not ignored but, rather, emphasized. However, his buildings do differ from postmodern grandchildren and great-grandchildren, in that Sullivan in the end believed in a resolution of opposites "by virtue of differential growth".

Peak and Decline

Due to the nation-wide economic recession, Adler & Sullivan recorded a 50 % drop in the number of commissions in 1892. This trend continued even after the overall situation began to improve. The only new commission in 1895 was the Guaranty Building in Buffalo, New York. Sullivan thought he could blame the Chicago World Exposition of 1893 for the downturn in business, claiming that it had released a "taste-virus" which festered quietly for a while in the Middle West, suddenly breaking out in a fever of eclecticism (Sullivan 1922/23, p. 322).

In July 1895, probably due to financial pressures, Adler retired from the firm. He was offered a job as a consulting engineer by the Crane Elevator Company. Dissatisfied with the work, however, he returned to the practice of his old profession before the year was out. He opened his own office which was first located on the second floor, then later on the sixth floor of the Auditorium Building. Although Sullivan continued to reside on the seventeenth floor of the same building, they had little contact with each other during the four remaining years of Adler's life. All attempts made by Frank Lloyd Wright to reconcile the former partners were unsuccessful. Apparantly Adler was deeply hurt because Sullivan had in his absence removed his name from the plans of the Guaranty Building, the last work designed by the partnership of Adler & Sullivan.

From the dissolution of the partnership in 1895 to the death of Adler in 1900, Sullivan's commissions were at least as numerous as his former partner's. If one considers the scope of the projects, Sullivan's were actually larger and more important. Between 1898/99, he worked on three major skyscrapers simultaneously (Bayard Building, Gage Building, Schlesinger & Mayer Department Store). Adler did none. At the time, Sullivan façades were considered a unique trademark for which consumer-oriented entrepreneurs were willing to pay a large fee. After a

dürfte mit finanziellen Sorgen zusammenhängen. Er ließ sich von einer Firma als beratender Ingenieur anstellen, war jedoch von dieser Tätigkeit wenig befriedigt und nahm bereits vor Ablauf eines Jahres seinen alten Beruf wieder auf. Sein Büro befand sich im zweiten, später im sechsten Geschoß des Auditorium Building, während Sullivan weiterhin im 17. Geschoß des Turmes residierte. Alle Versuche Frank Lloyd Wrights, die ehemaligen Partner wieder zusammenzubringen, waren erfolglos. Angeblich war Adler zutiefst verletzt, weil Sullivan in der Zwischenzeit seinen Namen auf den Plänen des Guaranty Building gelöscht hatte.

Nach Auflösung der Partnerschaft bis zum Tode Adlers im Jahre 1900 erhielt Sullivan nicht weniger Aufträge als sein ehemaliger Partner. Betrachtet man den Umfang der Projekte, so lag er sogar vorn, arbeitete er doch 1898/99 immerhin an drei größeren Geschäftsbauten gleichzeitig (Bayard- und Gage Building, Schlesinger & Mayer Departement Store). Sullivan-Fassaden galten als besonderes Markenzeichen, wofür konsumorientierte Unternehmen einen Aufpreis zu zahlen bereit waren. Nachdem sich eine Reihe junger Studenten daran machte, seine Ornamente zu kopieren, wurde bald von einem «sullivanesken Stil» gesprochen.

Nur kurze Zeit nachdem die Partnerschaft mit Adler aufgelöst worden war, erschien in der Serie «Great American Architects» eine umfangreiche Würdigung der Arbeit von Adler & Sullivan durch Montgomery Schuyler, den hervorragenden Kritiker von «Architectural Review» (1895). Sullivan rückte danach immer mehr in den Mittelpunkt von Architekturdebatten, bei denen seine theoretischen Abhandlungen und Kommentare zu eigenen Bauten gefragt waren. Zur Gründung der «Architectural League of America» (ALA) 1899 – als Alternative zum von Ostküstenarchitekten beherrschten «American Institute of Architects» (AIA) gedacht – übermittelte Sullivan einen Text mit dem Titel «The Modern Phase of Architecture». Die Lesung dieses Textes war das herausragende Ereignis des Kongresses, und sein Inhalt wurde zum programmatischen Eckpfeiler der Organisation erklärt. Ein Jahr später trat Sullivan persönlich vor den Delegierten des zweiten Kongresses der ALA auf, die sich im Auditorium Building in Chicago versammelt hatten. Er erntete frenetischen Beifall. Anschließend hielt Frank Lloyd Wright seinen Vortrag, den er mit den Worten begann: «Nachdem man dem Meister zugehört hat, scheint es wenig angemessen, dem Schüler zuzuhören.» (Twombly 1986, S. 365)

number of young students actually attempted to copy his ornament, people soon began to speak of a "Sullivanesque style".

Shortly after the partnership with Adler had ended, a comprehensive tribute to the work of Adler & Sullivan appeared in the series known as "Great American Architects" by Montgomery Schuyler, the outstanding critic of the "Architectural Review" (1895). After that, Sullivan became one of the main topics of architectural debates in which his theoretical treatises and personal comments on his own buildings were often discussed. In honor of the founding of the "Architectural League of America" (ALA) in 1899 – considered an alternative to the "American Institute of Architecture" (AIA) which was dominated by east coast architects – Sullivan delivered a paper entitled "The Modern Phase of Architecture". The presentation of it was the highlight of the conference. Its contents were immediately declared the programmatic cornerstone of the organization. A year later, Sullivan appeared in person to speak to the delegates of the second conference of the ALA who had gathered in the Auditorium Building in Chicago. The audience responded with overwhelming applause. Sullivan was followed by Frank Lloyd Wright who began his speech with the words: "after listening to the Master it hardly seems proper to listen to the disciple" (Twombly 1986, p. 365).

At the peak of his success as an outstanding and celebrated architect, as star of the ALA conference, Sullivan issued a series of polemic attacks against architectural education, the east coast establishment, and eclecticism. He did not even spare his followers and consequently lost the support of his friends within the ALA. In 1901/ 02, the 52 installments of his "Kindergarten Chats", up to that point Sullivan's most comprehensive theoretical treatise, were no longer published in the "Inland Architect", Chicago's leading architecture magazine. They appeared in the lesser known "Interstate Architect and Builder" where they were virtually ignored. In this text, Sullivan shifts suddenly from a suggestive artistic philosophy full of vague references, allusions, and building metaphors to harsh criticism of his supposed adversaries couched in the condescending tone of a pedantic schoolmaster.

In 1899, although she was twenty years younger than himself, Sullivan married Margaret Azona Hattabaugh from California. The couple usually spent several months of the year in their vacation cottage in Ocean Springs. In

Im Zenit seines Erfolgs als überragender und gefeierter Architekt, als Star der ALA-Kongresse steigerte sich Sullivan in eine Serie polemischer Ausfälle gegen Architektenausbildung, Ostküsten-Establishment, Eklektizismus, ohne dabei selbst seine Nachahmer zu schonen. Es gelang ihm schließlich nicht, seine Freunde innerhalb der ALA hinter sich zu halten. 1901/02 wurden die 52 Folgen von «Kindergarten Chats», bis zu diesem Zeitpunkt die umfangreichste theoretische Abhandlung Sullivans, nicht mehr in der führenden Chicagoer Architekturzeitschrift «Inland Architect» gedruckt, sondern im «Interstate Architect and Builder», wo sie praktisch nicht zur Kenntnis genommen wurden. In diesem Text wechselt Sullivan unvermittelt von «durch die Blume» gesprochenen Metaphern des Bauens über zu schulmeisterlicher Arroganz und Aggressionen gegen vermeintliche Widersacher.

Sullivan heiratete 1899 die um zwanzig Jahre jüngere, aus Kalifornien stammende Margaret Azona Hattabaugh. Das Paar verbrachte fortan mehrere Monate des Jahres im Ferienhaus in Ocean Springs. In Chicago wohnten die Sullivans zumeist in Dauerappartements von sehr guten Hotels, die sie innerhalb von zehn Jahren siebenmal wechselten. 1909 verschlechterten sich die Verhältnisse dramatisch. Die immer kleiner und spärlicher werdenden Aufträge reichten nicht mehr zur Finanzierung des bisherigen Lebensstils. Die letzte gemeinsame Wohnung lag in einer eher schlechten Gegend tief im Süden der Stadt (4300 Ellis Avenue). Ende des Jahres hatte Margaret genug von den alkoholischen Eskapaden ihres Gatten und verließ ihn. Nur wenige Tage zuvor hatte Sullivan seine Kunstsammlung und Bibliothek versteigert. Ebenso mußte er sein geliebtes Ferienhaus in Ocean Springs verkaufen. Er bezog in dieser Zeit ein Zimmer im billigen Warner Hotel an der Ecke Cottage Grove Avenue und 33. Straße, wo er bis zu seinem Tode blieb – an keinem andern Ort hatte er zuvor länger gewohnt als hier. Das Büro im obersten Geschoß des Turmes des Auditoriums konnte er bis 1918 halten, mußte dann in vier Räume auf dem zweiten Geschoß desselben Gebäudes wechseln, von wo er nach kurzer Zeit ausgewiesen wurde. Die letzten Projekte Sullivans entstanden in neuen Büros an der Prairie Avenue. Zudem hatte er einen Arbeitsplatz im Cliff Dwellers Club erhalten, wo er sein geistiges Vermächtnis niederschreiben konnte.

Inhaltlich fallen nach der Auflösung der Partnerschaft mit Adler einige thematische Verschiebungen in den theoreti-

Chicago, the Sullivans lived in suites of luxury hotels which they changed seven times in ten years. In 1909, due to a lack of commissions and ensuing financial trouble, their extravagant living standard plummeted. The last apartment they shared was located in a rather bad area in the south end of the city (4300 Ellis Avenue). By year-end, Margaret could no longer tolerate her spouse's alcoholic escapades and left him. Only a few days before, Sullivan had auctioned off his art collection and library. He was also forced to sell his beloved vacation cottage in Ocean Springs. He then moved into a room in the shoddy Warner Hotel on the corner of Cottage Grove Avenue and 33rd Street where he remained until he died – he lived here longer than he had in any one place in his entire life. He was able to retain his offices on the upper floor of the tower of the Auditorium Building until 1918. He then moved into four rooms on the second floor of the same building which he was soon forced to leave. Sullivan's last projects were executed in the new offices on Prairie Avenue. He retained, however, a place of work in the Cliff Dwellers Club where he recorded his intellectual and literary legacy.

Several thematic shifts are apparent in Sullivan's writings after the dissolution of the partnership with Adler. First, there were an increasing number of theoretical articles on structural problems, whereby Sullivan tried to escape the fate of being labeled merely a decorator. Secondly, Sullivan aligned himself with the new generation. Taking on the role of their spokesman, he addressed issues of education and architecture which culminated in his most famous work of this period: the "Kindergarten Chats". Thirdly, Sullivan expanded and refined his previous concept of function.

Sullivan had from the beginning not thought of function in purely quantifiable terms but rather, understood the complete inner disposition of a structure which was to be expressed in a outward form. In "What is Architecture" (1906), he broadened this view in accordance with Taine. Now Sullivan specifically included the system of thinking of a nation; thus, a building can be read as the biography of a culture: "as you are, so are your buildings" (Sullivan 1906, p. 186). It is perfectly possible that he was also inspired on this point by Victor Hugo who had developed similar ideas in "Notre Dame de Paris" (1832), particularly in the chapter entitled "Ceci tuera cela".

schen Beiträgen auf. Erstens entstanden vermehrt Texte über konstruktive Probleme, wodurch Sullivan der verhängnisvollen Festlegung auf die Rolle eines reinen Dekorateurs zu entkommen suchte. Zweitens verbündete sich Sullivan mit der neuen Generation, spielte sich als ihr Führer auf und diskutierte Fragen der Ausbildung. Höhepunkt in dieser Hinsicht stellen die «Kindergarten Chats» dar. Das dritte Thema ist demgegenüber nicht absolut neu: Sullivan ergänzt und präzisiert dabei seinen bisherigen Funktionsbegriff.

Unter «Funktion» hatte Sullivan von Anfang an nicht rein quantifizierbare Bedingungen verstanden, sondern die gesamte innere Disposition eines Bauwerks, welche in einer Gestalt auszudrücken war. In «What is Architecture» (1906) wurde diese Auffassung im Sinne von Taine erweitert. Als zur inneren Disposition eines Gebäudes gehörig behandelte Sullivan nun ausdrücklich auch die Denkart eines Volkes. Ein Bauwerk lasse sich als Buch des Lebens lesen: «Wie ihr seid, so sind eure Bauwerke» (Sullivan 1906, S. 186). Es ist durchaus möglich, daß er in diesem Punkt auch von Victor Hugo inspiriert war, der entsprechende Ideen in «Notre Dame de Paris» (1832), und dort speziell im Kapitel «Ceci tuera cela» entwickelte.

Das Problem der Funktion griff Sullivan erneut in «A System of Architectural Ornament According with a Philosophy of Man's Power» (1924) auf, obwohl dies auf den ersten Blick nicht zuzutreffen scheint. Denn auf den zwanzig Tafeln läßt er sich auf ein bizarres Spiel mit ornamentalen Formen nach Gesetzen einer nicht-euklidischen, «fließenden» Geometrie ein (siehe S. 163). Einzig durch die Tafel 9 wird die Folge der Zeichnungen unterbrochen: sie enthält eine allgemeine Erklärung über die Relevanz der übersteigerten Dekorationsformen. Unter dem Titel «Parallelismus-Lehre» kommt Sullivan hier auf die transzendentale Logik zu sprechen, derzufolge auch scheinbar getrennte Aktivitäten zu einem ganzheitlichen Phänomen verschmelzen: Eine universale Energie sei in allen Dingen vorhanden, welche der Künstler dank schöpferischer Kraft in seine Werke zu lenken vermöge. Die Schöpfungen des Menschen «sind Parallelen seiner selbst» (Sullivan 1924, S. 137). Dem erweiterten Parallelismusbegriff zufolge kann «Funktion» als jene universale Kraft verstanden werden, die Ausdruck in der Form sucht. Damit lieferte Sullivan eine philosophische Begründung seiner Formel «form follows function», nachdem er dies zuvor mit

Sullivan addressed the problem of functionality again in "A System of Architectural Ornament According with a Philosophy of Man's Power" (1924), a book of twenty very intricate and inventive illustrations. At first glance the concept of function does not seem to be relevant here, particularly because it seems that Sullivan gets involved in a bizarre game with ornamental forms according to the laws of a non-Euclidean fluid geometry (see p. 163). The sequence of drawings is only interrupted by the explanatory comments on plate 9 which contain a general explanation regarding the relevance of these spider web-like forms. Under the title "The Doctrine of Parallelism", Sullivan begins to discuss transcendental logic according to which even seemingly disparate activities fuse or blend into an integrated phenomenon. A universal energy is present in all things and only the artist, thanks to his creative powers, is able to direct it in his works of art: "his creations are but parallels of himself" (Sullivan 1924, p. 137). According to this expanded concept of parallelism, "function" can be understood as that universal force which is present in all things and seeks expression in form. After using physiognomical analogies and social-psychological arguments to explain his famous axiom in other articles, Sullivan finally offers a philosophical explanation of his formula "form follows function".

According to a compilation by Robert Twombly (1986), Sullivan received a total of 56 commissions from 1895 to 1924, although with a marked decrease in the number and size of the projects. From 1907 on, the only commissions he received were in the Middle West outside of Chicago. Despite difficulties in business and his personal life, Sullivan would make no concessions. He was more insistent than ever that his visions be precisely rendered in the form he dictated. Even in these financially hard times, he would not yield. He was more willing to lose a contract than to compromise his ideas. Dire necessity drove him, on the contrary, to be even more radical in his architectonic expression. Nevertheless, this radicalism expresses itself differently depending on the type of building – in this case, residences, department stores, or banks.

Out of a total of nine designs for residences, only the Babson House (1907) and the Bradley House (1909) were built. At first glance one notices, as with practically all of these projects, the characteristic features of the early

21 Frank Lloyd Wright: Robie
Residence, Chicago, 1906.

21 *Frank Lloyd Wright: Robie
Residence, Chicago, 1906.*

physiognomischen Analogien und sozial-psychologischen Argumenten getan hatte.

Nach einer Zusammenstellung von Robert Twombly (1986) erhielt Sullivan in der Zeit von 1895 bis 1924 insgesamt 56 Aufträge, allerdings mit stark abnehmender Tendenz was Anzahl und Größe der Projekte betrifft. Ab 1907 boten sich ihm nur noch im Hinterland von Chicago Gelegenheiten, seine Projekte auszuführen. Trotz geschäftlicher und persönlicher Schwierigkeiten machte Sullivan keine Konzessionen. Mehr denn je war er darauf erpicht, daß seine Visionen präzise umgesetzt wurden. Selbst in diesen Zeiten materieller Not blieb er unnachgiebig, eher bereit, einen Auftrag zu verlieren, als von seinen Ideen abzurücken. Die Not trieb ihn im Gegenteil zu einer oft mißverstandenen Radikalität des architektonischen Ausdrucks. Diesbezüglich lassen sich für Wohnbauten, Warenhäuser und Banken unterschiedliche Lösungsansätze unterscheiden.

Von den neun Entwürfen für Wohnbauten wurden nur das Haus Babson (1907) und das Haus Bradley (1909) ausgeführt. Hier, wie bei praktisch allen Projekten, fallen zunächst charakteristische Merkmale der frühen Phase der «Prairie School Architecture» auf: horizontaler Aufbau, Durchdringung von Bautrakten und Backsteinfassaden (Abbildung 21). Im Unterschied dazu jedoch behandelte Sullivan die Bauvolumen eher blockhaft und durchstieß die Fassade nur punktuell nach Maßgabe der dahinterliegenden Nutzung. Auch sind dekorative Elemente auf einzelne Partien verteilt und wirken wie auf nüchterne Baukörper aufgesetzte Schmuckstücke.

Am meisten wurde Sullivan in der letzten Periode von Aufträgen für Geschäftshäuser in Anspruch genommen. Von den 30 einschlägigen Aufträgen wurden immerhin rund die Hälfte gebaut. Dabei lassen sich zwei Gruppen unterscheiden. Die erste umfaßt die späten Geschäftshochhäuser zwischen 1897 und 1903, welche die Reihe der

phase of the "Prairie School of Architecture": horizontal composition, penetration of the different volumes and brick façades (Illustration 21). Yet Sullivan treated the volume of the building as a single rectilinear block, penetrating the façade only at certain points depending on the function of the space that lies behind it. In addition, the decorative elements are now clustered on individual parts of the building in such a way that they look like pieces of jewelery stuck-on to the otherwise bare façades.

In the last phase of his career, Sullivan was mostly involved with commissions for office buildings. Of the 30 commissions from this period, at least half were built. These buildings can be divided into two groups, the first one consisting of the late skyscrapers between 1897 and 1903 which continue the series of Adler & Sullivan's most famous buildings. Sullivan gradually moved away from his typical "all over" decorative treatment of the façades. Some elements are now distinct in terms of their degree of plasticity; for instance, the large figures of the angels under the roof cornice of the Bayard Building (1897–99), or the slender superimposed piers rising gracefully upward on the Gage (1898–99) or the Van Allen Building (1913–15), an opulent rendering of a model by Vaudremer (Illustration 22). On some buildings, the three parts were no longer unified in a classical sense, but articulated as distinct layers. These layers, which surround office or display windows like frames, are articulated with either restrained or lavish decoration depending on their purpose.

Between 1906 and 1920, Sullivan erected a total of eight bank buildings in various provincial towns in the Mid West. Beyond their immediate purpose as depositories for money, they symbolize a type of economic shrine with vaults in place of altars whose locking mechanisms protect the "secrets" of a secular faith. Sullivan's bank build-

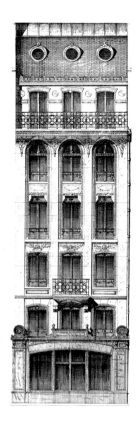

22 Emile Vaudremer:
Fassade an der Rue du Pont
Neuf, Paris.

22 *Emile Vaudremer: Façade,
Rue du Pont Neuf, Paris.*

berühmtesten Bauten von Adler & Sullivan fortsetzen. Sullivan kam dabei allmählich von den einheitlichen «all over»-Dekorationen an den Fassaden ab. Teils heben sich einzelne Elemente in plastischer Weise von andern ab, so etwa die Engelsfiguren unter dem Dachgesimse des Bayard Building (1897–99) oder aber die vorgeblendeten Stengel beim Gage (1898–99) und beim Van Allen Building (1913–15), die eine Vorgabe von Vaudremer auf opulente Art umsetzen (Abbildung 22). Teils wurden die verschiedenen Schichten nicht mehr zu einer Einheit zusammengefaßt, sondern als solche artikuliert und deutlich voneinander abgehoben. Diese Schichten sind wie Rahmen zu lesen, die sich zurückhaltend oder üppig um Büro- und Schaufenster schließen.

In der Zeit von 1906 bis 1920 entstanden in verschiedenen Provinzorten des Mittleren Westens insgesamt acht Bankgebäude. Über den unmittelbaren Zweck hinaus stellen sie eine Art von ökonomischen Heiligtümern dar, mit Tresors an Stelle von Altären, deren Verschlußmechanismen die «Geheimnisse» eines säkularisierten Glaubens bewahren. Sullivans Bankgebäude, die heute alle noch erhalten sind, bestehen hauptsächlich aus einem

ings, which are all still standing, consist mainly of one large central space subdivided by built-in enclosures and furniture. The small windows on the lower part of the façade, which refer to the division of the building plan, look like holes in the wall. On the other hand, the large openings located on the upper part which refer to the central lobby can no longer be read as such, simply because of their enormous size. They encompass the entire surface of the façade, so that the façade seems to surround the opening like a large frame. The sumptuous ornament serves to ally the actual window frames more closely with the wall. Sullivan himself had once called one of his bank buildings a "jewel box". This suggests an inter-relationship between inside and outside by making a correspondence between the exterior ornament and the value of the objects protected on the inside. In addition, Sullivan transformed this metaphor into a dominant architectonic theme in his designs by focusing particularly on the transitions between inside and outside. It seems, therefore, reasonable to assign ornament a symbolic function: for instance, in the case of the Grinell Bank (1913–14), where the interwoven frames surrounding

einzigen Großraum, der durch Einbauten von Brüstungen, Möblierungen und Trennwänden unterteilt wurde. Die kleinen Fenster der unteren Zone, die auf die Einteilung des Grundrisses Bezug nehmen, erscheinen wie in der Mauer ausgesparte Löcher. Die darüberliegenden großen Öffnungen dagegen, die sich auf den zentralen Schalterraum beziehen, können allein schon ihrer Größe wegen nicht mehr als solche gelesen werden. Sie nehmen die ganze Fassadenfläche in Anspruch, so daß diese wie ein großer Rahmen die Öffnung mit den farbigen Glasscheiben umschließt. Die üppigen Dekorationen dienen dazu, die eigentlichen Fensterrahmen mit der Fläche enger zu verbinden. Sullivan selbst hatte eines seiner Bankgebäude einmal als «Schmuckkästchen» bezeichnet, nicht zuletzt ist damit angedeutet, daß sich der äußere Schmuck und der Wert der innen aufbewahrten Dinge entsprechen. Sullivan verwandelte diese Beziehung in eine architektonische Metapher, indem er sich dabei vor allem auf die Übergänge zwischen Außen und Innen konzentrierte. Es liegt nahe, den Ornamenten deshalb auch eine symbolische Funktion zuzuweisen, etwa im Falle der Bank von Grinell (1913/14), wo die ineinander verschränkten Rahmen an den Verschlußmechanismus einer Kamera, aber auch an den des Banktresors denken lassen.

Autobiographie und Rezeption

Auf Veranlassung einiger Freunde zeichnete Sullivan seine Lebensgeschichte auf, der er den Titel «The Autobiography of an Idea» gab. Sie wurde in den Jahren 1922 und 1923 in monatlicher Folge im «Journal of the American Institute of Architects» publiziert. Der Herausgeber der Zeitschrift, Charles H. Whitaker, schlug schließlich auch eine Veröffentlichung als Buch vor, das dann 1924 erschien.

Der Inhalt dieser Autobiographie ist über die Erzählung der Lebensgeschichte hinaus bemerkenswert: Der 66jährige bricht seine Geschichte, in der dritten Person Singular geschrieben, in dem Moment ab, als er Partner von Dankmar Adler wurde und am Anfang einer großen Karriere stand. Die Zeit bis zum 15. Lebensjahr, als er in die Architekturabteilung des «Massachusetts Institute of Technology» (MIT) eintrat, nimmt rund die Hälfte des Buches ein. Bezeichnenderweise ist nur das letzte Kapitel der Autobiographie mit «Retrospect» überschrieben. Darin behan-

the window over the main entrance suggest the shutter mechanism in a camera or the locking mechanism of the vault inside the bank.

Autobiography and Critical Reception

Encouraged by several friends, Sullivan recorded the story of his life which he entitled "The Autobiography of an Idea". It was originally published in monthly issues in the "Journal of the American Institute of Architects" during 1922 and 1923. At the suggestion of the journal's editor, Charles H. Whitaker, it was also published in book form in 1924.

This autobiography, which is told in the third-person, is noteworthy beyond the simple narrative of Sullivan's life: Although written when Sullivan was over sixty-five, more than half of the book deals with Sullivan's youth up to his fifteenth year when he entered the Department of Architecture at the Massachusetts Institute of Technology. He abruptly ends his account at the moment he became partner with Dankmar Adler and was about to embark upon a great career. Interestingly enough, only the last of 15 chapters – entitled "Retrospect" – deals with the story of the heroic 1880s of Chicago architecture and the "misfortune" of the Chicago World's Fair of 1893. He wrote this retrospect, however, only at the suggestion of his publisher, who thought people should also read something about architecture after all the childhood memories.

Nonetheless, the attentive reader cannot help noticing that the entire book is really about architecture. This approach can be explained in that Sullivan associated "An Idea" with his "Autobiography"; in other words, as he wrote in a letter to Whitaker, this is his "philosophy of architecture". Again, this recalls Taine and his book "Philosophie de l'art". In effect, the autobiography does evolve according to Taine's theory as successive revelations of the fundamental force of the artist. "In childhood his idols had been big strong men who *did* things. Later on he had begun to feel the great power of men who could *think* things; later the expansive power of men who could *imagine* things; and at last (sic) he began to recognize as dominant, the will of the Creative Dreamer: he who possessed the power of vision to harness imagination, to harness the intellect, to make science do his will,

delt Sullivan die Geschichte der heroischen achtziger Jahre der Chicagoer Architektur und das «Unglück» der Weltausstellung von 1893. Geschrieben hat er diesen Rückblick allerdings erst nachträglich auf Anregung seines Verlegers, der meinte, die Leute müßten nach soviel Kindheitserinnerungen auch etwas über Architektur zu lesen bekommen.

Dem aufmerksamen Leser allerdings kann nicht entgehen, daß das ganze Buch von Architektur handelt. Sullivans Ansatz erklärt sich dadurch, daß er mit seiner Bildungsgeschichte eine Idee verknüpfte, genauer: seine «Philosophie der Architektur», wie er in einem Brief an Whitaker schrieb. Dies ruft nochmals Taine und dessen Buch «Philosophie de l'art» in Erinnerung. Tatsächlich entwickelt sich die Geschichte entsprechend dessen Theorie als sukzessive Enthüllung der grundlegenden Kraft des Künstlers. «In der Kindheit waren seine Idole starke Männer, die etwas *taten*. Später begann er die große Kraft zu spüren, die von jemandem ausging, der Dinge *denken* konnte; wieder später die enorme Macht von jemandem, der sich Dinge *vorstellen* konnte; zuletzt begann er den Willen des schöpferischen Träumers als übergeordnet zu erkennen: er, der allein die Macht der Vision besaß, mußte sich Vorstellungskraft, Denkvermögen, Wissenschaft und Gefühl – denn ohne Gefühl geht nichts – nutzbar machen.» (Sullivan 1922/23, S. 247) Diese Kraft selbst entdeckt zu haben, hält Sullivan für seine große persönliche Leistung und für das logische Produkt seiner Entwicklung. In welcher Form er diese Kraft in Bauten zu realisieren vermochte, hängt aber mit einem weiteren Topos zusammen, auf den er im Laufe der Erzählung immer wieder zurückgreift. Mehrmals schreibt Sullivan von den physiognomischen Zügen der Bauten, die ihm, dessen Augen nicht verdorben sind, ihre Geschiche erzählen. Er lernt, die Dinge nicht zum «Nennwert» zu nehmen und auch zwischen Funktion und Form, zwischen Innen und Außen zu unterscheiden (Sullivan 1922/23, S. 207). Damit ist der Schnittpunkt bestimmt, wo Sullivans Imagination ansetzt, um gemäß der Formel «form follows function» jedem Bauwerk seinen individuellen Ausdruck und jedem Problem seine eigene Lösung zu geben.

Als Sullivan am 14. April 1924 starb, war er verarmt, aber nicht vergessen. Letzteres ist insbesondere das Verdienst von Montgomery Schuyler, der häufig über Sullivans Arbeiten in «Architectural Record» berichtete und sie als wichtige Werke einer neuen Epoche verteidigte. Auf der-

to make the emotions serve him – for without emotion nothing" (Sullivan 1922/23, p. 247).

Sullivan considers the discovery of this fundamental force his greatest personal accomplishment and the logical product of his development. The form he gave his buildings is actually the outward expression of this force. This is, however, connected to another topos which he refers to again and again throughout his autobiography. Sullivan often writes of the physiognomical features of buildings that tell their story to one whose eyes are "not ruined". He learns not to take things at "face value" and also to distinguish between form and function, and between inside and outside (Sullivan 1922/23, p. 207). It is at this point that Sullivan's imagination takes over, extending his "power of vision" to give an individual expression to each building and to find an individual solution for each problem in accordance with the formula "form follows function".

When Sullivan died on April 14, 1924, he was poor but not forgotten. This was largely the to credit of Montgomery Schuyler, who frequently reported on Sullivan's projects in "Architectural Record", defending them as important works of a new era. Young critics and architects like Andrew N. Rebori, Thomas Tallmadge, and Claude Bragdon also argued along the same lines. Had Sullivan thought toward the end of his life that he had no decisive influence on the next generation, then this is true only for the great metropolitan centers of American cities. Nevertheless, the "Thirty-third Annual Chicago Architectural Exhibition" of 1902 presented a retrospective of Sullivan's work in a hall dedicated to the "Chicago School" amid many of his followers: including, among others Drummond, Maher, Pond & Pond, Purcell & Elmslie, Schmidt, Garden & Martin, Tallmadge & Watson (Wright was absent because he was in Japan at the time).

The response to Sullivan in Europe was naturally less, at least at first. Nevertheless, an article by none other than Hendrik P. Berlage appeared 1912 in the "Schweizerische Bauzeitung". Also, it is known that Adolf Loos – author of "Ornament and Crime" – had offered Sullivan the position of director of a private architecture school that he was planning to set up in Paris in 1920. The actual discovery of Sullivan in Europe came only after his death. Interest on the continent was first triggered by an "Exhibition of Modern American Architecture", which was shown in the "Akademie der Künste" in Berlin in 1926. Sullivan's work was honored by being exhibited in the main hall

selben Linie argumentierten auch jüngere Kritiker und Architekten wie Andrew N. Rebori, Thomas Tallmadge und Claude Bragdon. Wenn Sullivan gegen Ende seines Lebens von sich dachte, daß er ohne großen Einfluß auf die nachfolgende Generation geblieben ist, so mag dies mit Blick auf die Zentren der amerikanischen Großstädte zutreffen. Andererseits präsentierte die «Thirty-Third Annual Chicago Architectural Exhibition» von 1902 Sullivans Werk in einem der «Chicago School» gewidmeten Raum in extenso inmitten seiner Anhänger: unter andern waren dies Drummond, Maher, Pond & Pond, Purcell & Elmslie, Schmidt, Garden & Martin, Tallmadge & Watson (Wright fehlte, weil er sich zu dieser Zeit in Japan aufhielt).

In Europa war das Echo auf Sullivan naturgemäß vorerst schwächer. Immerhin erschien in der «Schweizerischen Bauzeitung» ein Bericht von keinem Geringeren als Hendrik P. Berlage (1912). Von Adolf Loos weiß man, daß er – Autor von «Ornament und Verbrechen» – für Sullivan die Leitung einer in Paris zu gründenden Privatschule für Architektur vorsah. Aber erst nach Sullivans Tod erfolgte dessen eigentliche Entdeckung in Europa. Ausgelöst wurde das Interesse durch eine 1926 in der Berliner «Akademie der Künste» gezeigte «Ausstellung neuerer amerikanischer Baukunst», wo Sullivan im wichtigsten Raum ausgestellt wurde (Abbildung 23). Ludwig Hilberseimer, Bruno Taut und etwas später Sigfried Giedion (1941) sahen in Sullivan den Vorläufer einer rational begründeten Auffassung von Architektur. Dabei blendeten sie geflissentlich die Ornamente aus und erhoben ihre (mechanistische) Interpretation von «form follows function» zum Dogma der Modernen Architektur. Auch die erste Monographie über Sullivan von Hugh Morrison (1935) ist hier einzuordnen, allerdings geht ihr Wert wegen der Fülle des Materials über rezeptionsgeschichtliche Aspekte hinaus.

In einer weiteren Phase der Sullivan-Rezeption ging es um die Integration Sullivans in die Tradition einer spezifisch amerikanischen Architektur (Mumford 1931, Condit 1951), ebenso in diejenige der amerikanischen Geistesgeschichte (Paul 1962). Im Gegenzug dazu wird heute eher die Verflechtung Sullivans mit der europäischen Kultur, insbesondere natürlich mit der École des Beaux-Arts ins Zentrum gerückt (van Zanten 1986). Dies hängt auch damit zusammen, daß innerhalb der Debatten um die Postmoderne Sullivans Ornamentik neue Aufmerksamkeit erlangte (Menocal 1981, Pollack 1987, Weingarden 1987).

(Illustration 23). Ludwig Hilberseimer, Bruno Taut, and, somewhat later, Sigfried Giedion (1941) saw Sullivan as a forerunner of a rationally based architecture. However, in so doing they deliberately ignored the ornament only to make their (mechanical) interpretation of "form follows function" the banner of the Modern Movement. The first monograph on Sullivan by Hugh Morrison (1935) is also to be classified here, though due to the wealth of material its value goes far beyond just an aspect of Sullivan's critical reception.

In a later phase of Sullivan's critical reception, efforts were made to integrate Sullivan into the American tradition (Mumford 1931, Condit 1951), as well as into the tradition of the history of the arts and humanities (Paul 1962). Today the focus is more on the inter-relationship of Sullivan and European culture, particularly regarding the Ecole des Beaux-Arts (van Zanten 1986). This shift in focus from America to Europe in his critical reception is partly due to the renewed attention that Sullivan's system of ornament has received within the debates surrounding the postmodern movement (Menocal 1981, Pollack 1987, Weingarden 1987).

This overview of the phases of the critical response to Sullivan's work shows that his buildings reveal many varied nuances depending on their context. One should not – to modify a well-known proverb – overlook the tree for the forest. My intent here is not to propose a cult of genius, yet the most remarkable feature of Sullivan's work is that it was created in opposition to the dominant mode of architecture at the time. Frank Lloyd Wright aptly expressed this aspect of Sullivan's "genius" in the title "Sullivan against the world", which he used as the heading of a draft of a chapter from "Genius and the Mobocracy". First of all, although Sullivan's education was Beaux-Arts oriented, he attacked nothing more vehemently in his entire life than that which the Beaux-Arts advocated style – imitation and an academic architecture dominated by historical forms. Secondly, although Sullivan is considered one of the most prominent representatives of the "Chicago School of Architecture", he surpassed all others in violating their law of rigorous sobriety. Thirdly, Sullivan wanted to establish a democratic and independent American architecture, yet it is precisely because of this that each of his buildings look like a buffalo in a herd of cattle. Sullivan was not an imitator, he was an agitator – he did not follow standards, he set his own standards. His architecture eludes categorization because

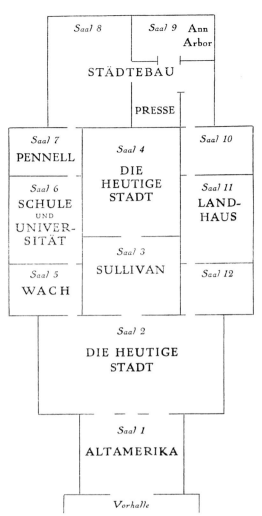

23 Raumdisposition der
«Ausstellung neuerer
amerikanischer Baukunst» in
der «Akademie der Künste»,
Berlin, 1926.

23 *Arrangement of the
exhibition "Ausstellung
neuerer amerikanischer
Baukunst" at the "Akademie
der Künste", Berlin, 1926.*

Dieser Überblick über die Rezeptionsgeschichte mag zeigen, daß Sullivans Werk je nach dem Kontext, in dem es dargestellt wird, in verschiedensten Nuancen aufleuchtet. Dabei darf man – um hier ein geläufiges Sprichwort abzuwandeln – vor lauter Wald den Baum nicht vergessen. Es soll hier nicht einem nebulösen Geniekult das Wort geredet werden, doch sollte man auch nicht vergessen, daß Sullivans Schaffen gegen alle Ströme seiner Zeit entstanden ist. Frank Lloyd Wright hat dies im Titel «Sullivan gegen die Welt» ausgedrückt, den er über den Vorabdruck eines Kapitels aus «Genius and the Mobocracy» setzte. Denn erstens: Sullivans Ausbildung war Beaux-Arts orientiert, endete denn auch folgerichtig im «Hauptquartier» derselben in Paris, und doch hat er sein Leben lang gegen nichts dermaßen polemisiert wie gegen Stil-

it is not a copy of an existing style but a unique creation – an endless poetic transformation and reinterpretation of existing forms. He applied the most modern technology without making it absolute; he was pragmatic, but never at the expense of poetics.

imitationen und das akademische Form-Diktat der Schulen. Zweitens: Sullivan zählt zu den prominentesten Vertretern der «Chicago School of Architecture», und doch hat er in einem nicht zu überbietenden Maße gegen deren Tendenz zu rigoroser Nüchternheit verstoßen. Und drittens: Sullivan wollte einen demokratischen und eigenständig amerikanischen Ausdruck in der Architektur durchsetzen, doch gerade deshalb nehmen sich seine Bauten aus wie Auerochsen in einer Kuhherde. Sullivans Sache war nicht Gefolgschaft, sondern Auseinandersetzung; seine Architektur paßt in keine Schublade, sondern besteht in einer unablässigen, poetischen Verwandlung und Umdeutung gegebener Formen. Er hat die modernste Technik angewandt, ohne sie zu verabsolutieren; er war pragmatisch, aber um keinen Preis auf Kosten der Poetik.

1 Der irische Nobelpreisträger von 1923, William B. Yeats, hat eine ähnliche Ununterscheidbarkeit im Gedicht «Among School Children» in der letzten Strophe ausgedrückt, wo es heißt: «O Kastanienbaum, großgewurzelter Blüher, / Bist Blatt du, Blüte oder Stamm? / O Leib, der zu Musik beschwingt, O glänzender Blick, / Wie können wir vom Tanz den Tänzer unterscheiden?»

2 Sullivan besaß eine dreibändige Ausgabe der «Physiognomischen Fragmente zur Beförderung der Menschenkenntnis und Menschenliebe» [«Essays on Physiognomy Designed to Promote the Knowledge and the Love of Mankind»] (1775–1778). Vergleiche dazu Pollak 1987, S. 260.

1 W. B. Yeats, who won the Nobel Prize in 1923, expressed a similar vision in the last stanza of his poem, *Among School Children*: "Oh chestnut tree, great-rooted blossomer, / Are you the leaf, the blossom or the bole? / O body swayed to music, O brightening glance, / How can we know the dancer from the dance?"

2 Sullivan owned the three-volume edition of "Essays on Physiognomy Designed to Promote the Knowledge and the Love of Mankind" (1775–1778). Cf. Pollak 1987, p. 260.

Bauten und Entwürfe

Buildings and Designs

Ornamente 1874–1876

Während Sullivan an der École des Beaux-Arts in Paris studierte, entstanden einige Dekorationsentwürfe, die er an einen ehemaligen Berufskollegen in Chicago schickte. In seinen Zeichnungen vermischten sich Spuren der Romantischen Schule, der damals avanciertesten Position an der Beaux-Arts, mit der Gestaltungsweise des «großen wilden Mannes der amerikanischen Architektur», Frank Furness, bei dem Sullivan vor seinem Pariser Aufenthalt für kurze Zeit gearbeitet hatte. Außerdem sind aus dieser Zeit auch Kopien nach Vorlagen von Vignola und Ruprich-Robert erhalten. Mitte 1875 kehrte Sullivan nach Chicago zurück, wo er sich zunächst als Dekorateur von sakralen Innenräumen (Moody's Tabernacle und Sinai Temple) einen Namen machte.

Architectural Ornament 1874–1876

While studying at the École des Beaux-Arts in Paris, Sullivan sketched several ornamental designs which he later sent to a former colleague in Chicago. Traces of the romantic school, which ranked number one at that time at the Beaux-Arts, were combined with formal elements of the "famous wild man of American architecture", Frank Furness, with whom Sullivan had collaborated shortly before going to Paris. Adaptations of designs by Vignola and Ruprich Robert dating from the same period exist as well. Sullivan returned to Chicago in 1875, where he began to establish himself as a decorator of ecclesiastical interiors (Moody's Tabernacle and the Sinai Temple).

Sullivans Zeichnung für
John Edelmann in Chicago,
29. November 1874,
Tusche auf Skizzenpapier,
26,5 × 41,3 cm.
*Sullivan's drawing for
John Edelmann in Chicago,
November 29th 1874, ink on
tracing paper, 26,5 × 41,3 cm.*

Sullivans Entwurf für eine
Deckenuntersicht, Mai 1876,
Tusche auf Papier,
40 × 73,5 cm.
*Sullivan's design for a ceiling,
ink on paper, 40 × 73,5 cm.*

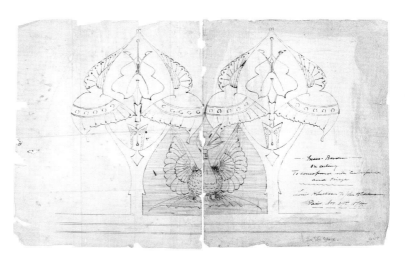

Central Music Hall   1878–1880

Randolph und State Streets, Chicago; 1901 abgerissen

Einflußreiche Geschäftsleute aus Chicago unterstützten das Projekt, unter andern auch Martin Ryerson und Ferdinand W. Peck, die später wichtige Aufträge an Adler & Sullivan vergaben. Der Saal wurde von der Central Church sowohl für liturgische Zwecke als auch für Konzerte genutzt und bot 1900 Personen Platz. Seine Akustik galt als hervorragend. Dankmar Adler legte damit die Grundlage für die künftigen Erfolge seines Büros. Kommerzielle Nutzungen (12 Läden, 75 Büros und zwei kleinere Vortragssäle) schirmten den Saal vom Straßenlärm ab. Sullivan begann erst nach der offiziellen Eröffnung, Ende 1879, an diesem Projekt zu arbeiten: er war, entsprechend seinen Vorlieben, für die Dekoration des großen Saals verantwortlich.

Central Music Hall   1878–1880

Randolph and State Streets, Chicago; demolished in 1901

This project was financed by influential Chicago businessmen, including Martin Ryerson and Ferdinand W. Peck who later awarded Adler & Sullivan other important commissions. Well-known for its superb acoustics, the concert hall, with a seating capacity of 1900, was used by the Central Church for liturgical purposes as well as concerts. The six-story structure also contained commercial space (12 stores, 75 offices, and two smaller lecture halls) which blocked out the street noise. This music hall, Dankmar Adler's first independent architectural undertaking, established the professional reputation and subsequent success of his firm, particularly in the field of acoustics. Shortly after joining Adler as a draftsman in 1879, Sullivan began working on this project which was officially opened in December of that year. In accordance with his predilection, Sullivan was responsible for the decorative organ grilles in the large auditorium.

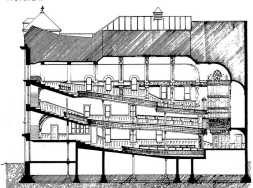

Längsschnitt.
Longitudinal section.

Bühne mit Orgel.
Proscenium and Organ.

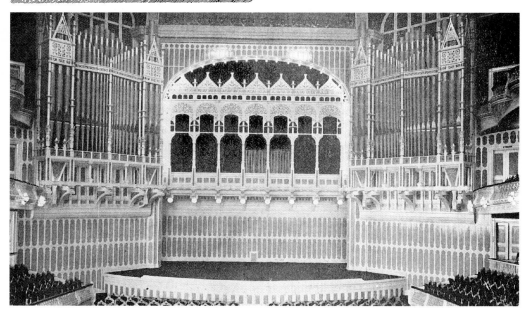

Rothschild Building   1880/81

210 West Monroe Street, Chicago ; 1972 abgerissen
Der Geschäftsbau wurde für das Kleidergeschäft von
Emanuel Rothschild & Brothers errichtet. Die über 15 Meter breite Fassade besaß drei durchgehende schlanke
Mauerwerkpfeiler, die die dazwischenliegenden Fassaden aus Glas und Gußeisen trugen. Die stilisierten Ornamente lösten sich gegen oben von ihrer reliefartigen Prä-
gung der Fassade, traten plastischer in Erscheinung,
bis sie schließlich in einer Art «zurechtgestutzter floraler
Skyline» (van Zanten 1986, S. 13) endeten.

Rothschild Building   1880/81

210 West Monroe Street, Chicago ; demolished in 1972
This office building was erected for the clothing firm of
Emanuel Rothschild & Brothers. Three narrow continuous
masonry piers divided the façade, which was 50 feet
wide, into two glass and cast-iron bays. The flat surface
quality of the ornamental reliefs on the lower part of the
façade became increasingly stylized and three-dimen-
sional with each successive floor, ending finally in a high
degree of plasticity that evoked a kind of "cut-out floral
skyline" (van Zanten 1986, p. 13).

Ansicht der Frontfassade.
View of the main elevation.

Borden Block   1880–1882

Nordwestecke Randolph und Dearborn Streets, Chicago;
1916 abgerissen

Adlers autobiographischen Aufzeichnungen zufolge war
dies der erste Bau, den er in «Zusammenarbeit mit
Mr. Sullivan» ausführte. Er kann in konstruktiver Hinsicht
mit dem Ersten Leiter Building (1879) von W. L. B. Jenney
verglichen werden, welches nur wenige Monate früher errichtet worden ist und welches als das erste Gebäude der
«Chicago School of Architecture» gilt. In beiden Fällen
wurde das vom Chicagoer Ingenieur Baumann entwik-
kelte System der Einzelfundamentierung angewendet.
Doch während beim Borden Block die Öffnungen nur so-
weit vergrößert werden konnten, als die gemauerten Pfeiler die Last der gußeisernen Fensterstürze aufzunehmen
vermochten, verstärkte Jenney bei seinem Gebäude die
Pfeiler innen mit gußeisernen Pilastern. Er erreichte dadurch eine bedeutend höhere Tragfähigkeit, was ihm größere Spannweiten der Öffnungen erlaubte. In formaler
Hinsicht jedoch zeigten sich beim Borden Block neue An-
sätze: hier wurden die einzelnen Geschosse nicht einfach
– wie allgemein üblich – gestapelt, sondern in eine einheitliche Komposition des Ganzen eingebunden.

Borden Block   1880–1882

Northwest corner of Randolph and Dearborn Streets,
Chicago; demolished in 1916

According to Adler's autobiographical notes, this was the
first building that he constructed in "collaboration with
Mr. Sullivan". Structurally comparable to the First Leiter
Building (1879) built by W. L. B. Jenney only a few months
earlier, the Borden is considered to be the first building of
the "Chicago School of Architecture". Both buildings
used the new system of isolated pier foundations for wall
support developed by the Chicago engineer Baumann.
Although the Borden was a departure from solid-wall
construction, the span of the openings was still limited
by the strength of the weight-bearing masonry piers used
to support the cast-iron lintels over the windows. Jenney, on the other hand, achieved a significantly higher
load-bearing capacity in his building by reinforcing the
weight-bearing masonry piers with cast-iron pilasters,
thus making a greater widening of the openings possible. Formally, however, the Borden did exemplify structural innovations: the individual stories were not simply
stacked on top of each other – which was common at
the time – but integrated into the design as a whole.

Straßenfassaden, im
Hintergrund das Schiller
Building von Adler & Sullivan
(vergleiche Seite 90).
*Street elevations, at the
background the Schiller
Building of Adler & Sullivan
(see also page 90).*

Haus Borden   1880

3949 Lake Park Avenue, Chicago; abgerissen

Der Stil der französischen «Romantischen Schule» (Duban, Duc, Labrouste, Vaudoyer u. a.) zeichnete sich durch eine betont flächige Auffassung der Fassade aus sowie durch Schmuckformen, die einer Mischung aus ägyptischen und mittelalterlichen Motiven entsprachen und reliefartig in den Stein eingeritzt wurden. Dieser Stil begann sich um die Mitte des 19. Jahrhunderts auch außerhalb der Beaux-Arts durchzusetzen. Er entsprach auch dem Geschmack einer gehobenen Klientel, die sich seit den siebziger Jahren vorzugsweise südlich des Geschäftszentrums von Chicago anzusiedeln begann. Er wurde dort vom New Yorker Architekten und ersten amerikanischen Absolventen der Beaux-Arts, Morris R. Hunt, mit dem Wohnhaus für Marshall Fields (1871–1873) eingeführt. Einheimische Architekten wie Burnham & Root oder Adler (schon vor seiner Zusammenarbeit mit Sullivan) folgten seinem Beispiel.

Borden Residence   1880

3949 Lake Park Avenue, Chicago; demolished

The style of the French romantic school (Duban, Duc, Labrouste, Vaudoyer, etc.) began to gain acceptance during the middle of the nineteenth century even outside of the École des Beaux-Arts. It is characterized by an emphasis on flat surface articulation of the façade as well as by ornament that combines Egyptian and medieval forms carved into the surface like a relief. This style suited the taste of an upper-class clientele who had begun in the 70's to settle in an area just south of the business district of Chicago. Morris Hunt, the New York architect and first American graduate of the Beaux-Arts, introduced this style to Chicago with his Marshall Field's residence (1871–1873). American architects like Burnham & Root or Adler (even before collaboration with Sullivan) soon followed suit.

Ansicht von der Straße aus.
View from the street.

Jewelers' Building   1881/82

15–19 South Wabash Avenue, Chicago;
im Erdgeschoß stark verändert

Der erste von insgesamt sechs Aufträgen von Martin A. Ryerson (vergleiche Revell Building, Ryerson Building und Walker Building). Die Komposition der fünfgeschossigen Fassade beruht einerseits auf der großflächigen Zusammenfassung von Öffnungen über mehrere Geschosse im Mittelteil und andererseits auf den vertikalen Akzenten der beiden flankierenden Joche. Auch diese Gestaltungsweise läßt sich mit Beispielen zeitgenössischer Pariser Boulevard-Architektur in Verbindung bringen.

Jewelers' Building   1881/82

15–19 South Wabash Avenue, Chicago;
1st floor extensively remodelled

This was the first of a total of six commissions for Martin A. Ryerson (cf. Revell Building, Ryerson Building and Walker Building). The five-story façade is composed of a large window grouping at the center connecting several floors flanked by two narrow vertical bays. This design also recalls contemporary boulevard architecture in Paris.

4. und 5. Geschoß der Frontfassade, Photo von Richard Nickel.
4th and 5th floor street elevation, Photo by Richard Nickel.

Revell Building   1881–1883

Nordostecke Adams und Wabash Streets, Chicago;
1968 abgerissen

Das Fassadenschema des Jewelers' Building mit seiner
Abfolge unterschiedlicher Joche wurde übernommen und
erweitert. Die Ornamente waren nicht tektonisch, sondern erschienen als bloß oberflächliche Ritzungen. Die
Tragkonstruktion im Innern bestand aus eisernen Stützen
und Trägern, die nach einem Patent des Architekten Peter
B. Wight mit Tonplatten verkleidet wurden. Dank diesen
überstand das Gebäude 1902 einen Brand.

Revell Building   1881–1883

Northeast corner of Adams and Wabash Streets, Chicago;
demolished in 1968

The scheme of the façade with its successive bays of unequal sizes is basically an extension of the design found
on the Jewelers' Building. The purpose of the ornament
was not tectonic; it was merely a flat incised surface pattern. The interior load-bearing structure consisted of iron
columns and girders sheathed in terra-cotta tiles, a
patented fireproofing process developed by the architect
Peter B. Wight. Thanks to this new technique, the building survived a fire in 1902.

Photo von J. W. Taylor.
Photo by J. W. Taylor.

Haus Halsted   1883

440 West Beldon Street, Chicago

Das Wohnhaus für Ann Halsted liegt nördlich des Geschäftszentrums von Chicago in einem Gebiet, wo sich mittelständische Familien niederließen. Die fast schmucklosen Fassaden aus rötlichem Backstein und die Segmentbögen über den Öffnungen sind Merkmale, die auch im damaligen Industriebau zu finden sind (vergleiche Brunswick-Fabrik, S. 102).

Halsted Residence   1883

440 West Beldon Street, Chicago

The residence built for Ann Halsted is situated north of the business district of Chicago in an area largely inhabited by middle-class families. The simple, almost unadorned façade made of red brick, as well as the segmental arches above the bays, are features which are also found on industrial buildings of that era. (Cf. Brunswick Factory, p. 102).

Photo von Richard Nickel.
Photo by Richard Nickel.

Haus Selz, Haus Schwab   1883

1717 und 1715 Michigan Avenue, Chicago; abgerissen
Der Bau der beiden benachbarten Wohnhäuser wurde unabhängig voneinander abgewickelt, obwohl Morris Selz
und Charles H. Schwab geschäftlich liiert waren. Mit
30 000 Dollar kostete das Selz-Haus etwa doppelt so viel
wie das Wohnhaus für Ann Halsted. Verglichen mit andern Villen an der «millionaires row», wie die Michigan
Avenue zwischen den Nummern 1700 und 1900 genannt
wurde, war diese Bausumme immer noch sehr beschei-
den. Später wurden Adler & Sullivan auch für den Bau der
Fabrik von Selz und Schwab engagiert.

Selz Residence, Schwab Residence   1883

1717 and 1715 Michigan Avenue, Chicago; demolished
These two adjacent residences were built independently,
even though Morris Selz and Charles H. Schwab worked
together as business partners. At a sum of 30 000 dollars,
the Selz house was twice as expensive as the Ann Halsted
residence. Compared to other villas on "millionaire's
row", as the 1700–1900 block on Michigan Avenue was
called, this was still a modest sum. Adler & Sullivan were
also engaged a few years later to design the factory building of Selz & Schwab, Co.

Rechts Haus Selz, links Haus Schwab.
Right Selz Residence, left Schwab Residence.

Reihenhäuser für Ann Halsted   1884,
Anbau   1885

1826–1834 Lincoln Park West, Chicago

Dach- und Sohlbankgesimse fassen die fünf Wohneinheiten zusammen. Zum einen aber unterscheiden sich Haus Nr. 2 und Nr. 4 bezüglich Fenster- und Schmuckformen von den benachbarten Einheiten. Zum andern überspielen kantige Profile über einzelnen Öffnungen im Erdgeschoß die funktionelle Teilung und bilden Symmetrieachsen, die je zwei Häuser zusammenbinden. Die Gestaltung dieser Profile erinnert an neogotische Bauten von Viollet-le-Duc in Paris.

Residences for Ann Halsted   1884,
Addition   1885

1826–1834 Lincoln Park West, Chicago

A continuous roof cornice and string course under the windows connect these five single dwellings. The windows and the ornament on house No. 2 and house No. 4 are markedly different from the adjacent houses (Nos. 1, 3 and 5), but the angular mouldings above the individual openings on the first floor counter the functional division between houses. The symmetrical axes formed by these mouldings thus serve to join adjacent houses. The treatment of these mouldings is reminiscent of neo-gothic buildings by Viollet-le-Duc in Paris.

Grundrisse (mit späteren Änderungen) und Straßenfassade.
Floor plans (with later alterations) and street elevation.

Eugène Viollet-le-Duc: Maison Courmont in Paris,
1846–1849.
Eugène Viollet-le-Duc: Maison Courmont in Paris,
1846–1849.

Photo von Richard Nickel.
Photo by Richard Nickel.

Ryerson Building   1884

16–20 East Randolph, Chicago; abgerissen

Die tragenden Teile der Frontfassade waren aus hellem Bedford-Sandstein, Seiten- und Rückfassaden aus Backstein. Das innere Traggerüst aus Eisen wurde vollständig mit leichten Tonplatten gegen Feuer geschützt. Zum ersten Mal fanden sich bei einem Geschäftshaus großzügig verglaste Erker, um die natürliche Belichtung der Räume zu verbessern. Diese «bay windows» wurden in der Folge zu einem der signifikanten Merkmale des frühen Stils der «Chicago School of Architecture». Die bissig-scharfe Bemerkung von John W. Root vom Jahre 1887, wonach Sullivan ganze Fassaden mit Ornamenten zugekleistert habe, trifft am ehesten auf dieses Gebäude zu. Entsprechend den Prinzipien der «Romantischen Schule» wurden die Dekorationen absichtlich von konstruktiver Bedingtheit getrennt und – teils abgeleitet von weit auseinanderliegenden Inspirationsfeldern – geometrisch stilisiert.

Ryerson Building   1884

16–20 East Randolph, Chicago; demolished

The load-bearing elements of the front façade consisted of light Bedford sandstone; the side and back façades were of brick. The interior frame of iron was completely sheated in light fire-resistant terra-cotta tiles. Large bay windows were used for the first time on an office building to increase the amount of natural light in the rooms. Later, bay windows became a significant feature of the early style of the "Chicago School of Architecture". John W. Root's vicious remark made in 1887, claiming that Sullivan was going to "smear another façade with ornament", applies best to this building. Following the principles of the romantic school, ornament was intentionally separated from structural necessity and – derived in part from completely unrelated sources of inspiration – geometrically stylized.

Zeichnung der Frontfassade.
Drawing of the main elevation.

Troescher Building   1884

15–19 South Market Street, Chicago; abgerissen
Die vertikale Einheit der Fassade ist beim Troescher Build-ing überzeugender gelöst worden als bei allen andern fünf- und mehrgeschossigen Bauten, die bis zu diesem Zeitpunkt in Chicago entstanden waren. Die Dreiteilung (Sockel, Schaft und Dach) und die durchgehenden Back-steinpfeiler im mittleren Teil der Fassade wiesen bereits auf die Komposition des Wainwright Building (1890/91) in St. Louis hin.

Troescher Building   1884

15–19 South Market Street, Chicago; demolished
The vertical unity of the façade of the Troescher Building was more convincingly and successfully solved than any other building of five stories or more that had been built up to that time in Chicago. The tripartite division (base, shaft and roof) and the continuous brick piers in the mid-dle section (shaft) of the façade anticipate the design of the Wainwright Building (1890/91) in St. Louis.

5. und 6. Geschoß der Frontfassade, Photo von Richard Nickel.
Photo of the 5th and 6th floor main elevation by Richard Nickel.

McVicker's Theater, Umbauten   1883–1885 und 1890/91

25 West Madison Street, Chicago; 1925 abgerissen
Das kurz nach dem großen Brand von Chicago (1871) errichtete Gebäude wurde von der Firma Adler & Sullivan, die sich im Mai 1883 konstituierte, straßenseitig um zwei Bürogeschosse erhöht. Der Saal wurde für ein Fassungsvermögen von 2000 Zuschauern ausgebaut und mit entsprechenden akustischen Verbesserungen versehen. Die Heizungs- und Belüftungsanlage kostete die damals respektable Summe von 6000 Dollar, was etwa 7% der gesamten Baukosten ausmachte. Kalte oder warme Luft wurde von der Decke herabgeblasen und unter den Sitzplätzen wieder abgesaugt. Das Belüftungssystem wurde gleichzeitig als «Schallträger» genutzt (Wright 1949, S. 66). Anläßlich der Eröffnung gaben die Dekorationen des Saals mehr als alles andere zu reden. Sullivan als «designing partner» ließ angeblich 1235 elektrische Glühbirnen – dies nur sechs Jahre nachdem die Edison Electric Co. mit deren Produktion begonnen hatte – ohne Lampenschirm direkt in die floralen Stukkaturen einsetzen.

Im August 1890 zerstörte ein Feuer die Ausstattungen. Wiederum erhielten Adler & Sullivan den Auftrag, und wiederum wurde aus dem Umbau de facto ein Neubau: Neue Eisenträger über dem Zuschauerraum trugen die Erweiterungen der beiden obersten Bürogeschosse. Die Kapazität des Saals wurde um 165 Plätze reduziert, seine Dekoration vollständig neu konzipiert. Die Reliefs über den Zuschauer-Boxen neben der Bühne stammten von Johann Gelert, der sich 1887 in Chicago niedergelassen und unter anderem auf dekorative Skulpturen spezialisiert hatte.

McVicker's Theater, Remodelling   1883–1885 and 1890/91

25 West Madison Street, Chicago; demolished in 1925
The firm of Adler & Sullivan, founded in May 1883, remodelled McVicker's Theater – built after the great fire in Chicago (1871) – by adding two stories of office space facing the street. The auditorium was also remodelled and enlarged to hold 2000 spectators; there were corresponding acoustic improvements. The heating and ventilation system cost the then respectable amount of 6000 dollars, approximately 7% of the total construction costs. Ventilation ducts in the ceiling circulated warm or cold air to the numerous air outlets under the seats. The ventilation system also served simultaneously "to carry sound" (Wright 1949, p. 66). On opening night, the architectural ornament created an uproar: Sullivan, now considered the "designing partner" of the firm, had embedded 1235 bare light bulbs – just six years after Edison Electric Co. had started production – into the ornamental plaster reliefs decorated with intricate floral and foliate patterns.

The interior was destroyed by fire in August 1890. Adler & Sullivan were again awarded the commission, but instead of remodelling they actually designed a totally new interior: new iron girders above the parquet supported the extensions on the two uppermost floors of offices. The capacity of the auditorium was reduced by 165 seats and the ornament was completely redesigned. The large reliefs above the proscenium boxes were done by Johann Gelert who moved to Chicago in 1887, where he specialized in, among other things, ornamental sculpture.

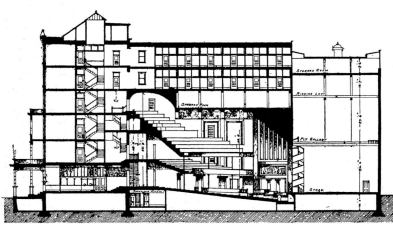

Längsschnitt des Projekts, 1891.
Longitudinal section of the project, 1891.

Zeichnung des Vestibüls, 1885.
Drawing of the vestibule, 1885.

Proszenium und Relief nach 1891.
Proscenium and relief after 1891.

Chicago Opera Festival Hall   1885

Michigan Avenue, Chicago; abgerissen

Der wichtigste Mäzen von Chicagos Musikleben, der Geschäftsmann Ferdinand W. Peck, initiierte 1885 ein großes Opernfestival. Zu diesem Zwecke wurde das bestehende Interstate Exposition Building, das 1873 nach Plänen von W. W. Boyington erbaut worden war, vollständig neu eingerichtet. Die großen, trichterförmig angeordneten Schalen, die Adler aus akustischen Gründen an die Bühnenöffnung ansetzte, ließ Sullivan mit riesigen Ornamenten schmücken, deren flächige Komposition an den Stil von Frank Furness erinnerte. Im Saal fanden 6200 Zuhörer Platz. Das Ausstellungsgebäude mußte schon 1892 dem Bau des Art Institute of Chicago weichen.

Chicago Opera Festival Hall   1885

Michigan Avenue, Chicago; demolished

Ferdinand W. Peck, businessman as well as the most influential patron of the Chicago music scene, conceived of the idea of a large opera festival. The existing Interstate Exposition Building, erected in 1873 by W. W. Boyington, was completely remodelled to house the temporary structure. Adler used large ceiling panels arranged in the shape of a funnel as the basis of the design of the vaulted ceiling. These panels, placed directly above the stage opening for acoustic reasons, were decorated by Sullivan with gigantic ornaments, whose flat two-dimensional design was reminiscent of the style of Frank Furness. The auditorium could seat 6200 people. In 1892 the exposition building was torn down to erect the Art Institute of Chicago.

Zeichnung des dekorierten Saals.
Drawing of the decorated hall.

Rechte Seite: Ansicht des Proszeniums.
Right page: View of the proscenium.

Dexter Building   1887

630 South Wabash Avenue, Chicago

Das für Wirt Dexter errichtete Geschäftshaus im südlichen Teil des Zentrums von Chicago entspricht weitgehend dem Schema, das Sullivan in den frühen achtziger Jahren für diesen Bautypus entwickelt hatte. Geschlossene und offene Partien, schmale und weite Joche, Konstruktionen aus Mauerwerk und aus Gußeisen sind zu einer Einheit komponiert. Durch diesen Bau erzielten Adler & Sullivan ihre größte Übereinstimmung mit dem nüchternen «Chicago Commercial Style», der später zum Inbegriff der «Chicago School of Architecture» wurde.

Dexter Building   1887

630 South Wabash Avenue, Chicago

Erected for Wirt Dexter in the southern part of downtown Chicago, this building corresponds almost entirely to the design scheme developed by Sullivan for office building in the early 1880s. Enclosed and open spaces, narrow and wide bays, and masonry and cast-iron structures have been designed to form a coherent whole. In this building Adler & Sullivan came closest to the sober "Chicago Commercial Style", later becoming the epitome of the "Chicago School of Architecture".

Photo von Richard Nickel.
Photo by Richard Nickel.

Grabmal für Martin A. Ryerson   1887

Graceland Cemetery, Chicago

Das Grabmal für einen der wichtigsten Auftraggeber von Adler & Sullivan zeigt Sullivans architektonisches Denken unter neuen Voraussetzungen, nämlich ohne funktionelle und konstruktive Einschränkungen. Die glatt geschliffenen schwarzen Granitblöcke erinnern an ägyptische Mastabas und verleihen dem Grab einen Hauch von Ewigkeit. Dieser scheint sich zu verflüchtigen, wenn man die asymptotische Krümmung beachtet, in der das Gebäude wie ein orientalisches Zelt vom Boden aufsteigt. Solchermaßen werden zwei verschiedene Bautypen metaphorisch in der Form eines «steinernen Zeltes» zusammengebracht.

Tomb for Martin A. Ryerson   1887

Graceland Cemetery, Chicago

Designed for one of Adler & Sullivan's most important clients, the Ryerson tomb shows Sullivan's architectonic thinking under new circumstances, without functional and structural requirements. The smoothly polished black granite blocks which recall Egyptian mastabas lend the grave a hint of eternity. This effect seems to vanish when one looks at the asymptotic curve, in which the building rises up like an oriental tent. Two different types of buildings are thus metaphorically fused in the shape of a "stone tent".

Photo von Henry Fuermann.
Photo by Henry Fuermann.

Chicago Auditorium Building   1886–1889

Michigan und Wabash Avenues, Congress Street, Chicago

Der Erfolg des Festivals im Jahre 1885 ermutigte Ferdinand W. Peck und seine Freunde, der Oper in Chicago ein permanentes Haus einzurichten. Es handelte sich um den bisher größten Theaterbau Amerikas. Um das Vorhaben finanziell abzusichern, sollte dem Auditorium ein luxuriöses Hotel sowie ein Bürotrakt angegliedert werden. Ausschlaggebend für die Vergabe an Adler & Sullivan war deren Erfahrung in akustischen Angelegenheiten.

Die Direktoren der «Chicago Grand Auditorium Association» verlangten von Adler & Sullivan eine ähnliche äußere Gestaltung des Bauvolumens wie die des Marshall-Fields-Warenhauses (Adler 1892, S. 416). Sein Architekt war Henry Hobson Richardson, der kurz vor Vollendung dieses vielbeachteten Bauwerks im Mai 1886 bloß 47jährig starb. Adler & Sullivan modifizierten jedoch die Vorgabe: statt bossierten Granits verwendeten sie im oberen Teil der Fassade geschliffenen Sandstein, in den sie die Gewände der rundbogigen Öffnungen mehrstufig abgetreppt einließen. Dies ist neben der Gestaltung des Turmes der deutlichste Hinweis auf formale Lösungen der «Romantischen Schule». Als im Januar 1887 die Fundamente gelegt wurden, gab es nachträglich noch bedeutende Veränderungen am Bauprogramm. Insbesondere kam ein großer Speisesaal im zehnten Geschoß mit Sicht auf den Lake Michigan hinzu, zudem ein Bankettsaal, dessen 600 Tonnen Gewicht auf zwei Trägern von fast 35 Metern Spannweite über dem Auditorium ruhen. Weitere bautechnische Probleme verursachten der hohe Grundwasserspiegel ebenso wie die wegen seines «Übergewichts» zu erwartende größere Setzung des Turmes. Dieses Problem löste Adler, indem er das Fundament des Turmes zunächst mit dem Übergewicht vorbelastete, um dieses Gewicht dann sukzessive zu entfernen, als man den Turm über das zehnte Geschoß hochführte. Die Form des Zuschauerraums wurde abermals durch akustische Schalen bestimmt. Bei normalem Konzertbetrieb können 4237 Personen im Saal Platz nehmen. Mit beweglichen Decken- und Bodenelementen läßt sich die Kapazität stufenweise auf 2574 Sitze verringern respektive für Kongresse auf 7000 erhöhen. Allein die Größe des Projekts machte Pionierleistungen bezüglich Bühnenmechanismus, Klimatisierung und Energiegewinnung notwendig. Seinen bedeutenden Stellenwert innerhalb der Geschichte der modernen Architektur verdankt das Audito-

Chicago Auditorium Building   1886–1889

Michigan and Wabash Avenues, Congress Street, Chicago

The great success of the opera festival in 1885 prompted Ferdinand W. Peck and his friends to erect a permanent building for the Chicago Opera. This was to be the largest theater building ever erected in America. A luxurious hotel and an office block were added to the auditorium, to make the project more financially secure. Adler & Sullivan were selected for the project because of their expertise in acoustics.

Adler & Sullivan were urged by the directors of the "Chicago Grand Auditorium Association" to design an exterior façade along the lines of the Marshall Field Wholesale Store (Adler 1892, p. 416). Shortly before its completion, the architect of this renowned structure, Henry Hobson Richardson, died prematurely in May 1886. He was only 47 years old. Nevertheless, Adler and Sullivan did modify this guideline: rough-hewn granite was replaced by polished sandstone in the upper portion of the façade. This surface was articulated with round-arched openings whose jambs are recessed in steps from the wall plane. The treatment of the façade as well as the tower allude to formal solutions of the romantic school.

As the foundation was being built in January 1887, several significant changes were made in the building plan. In particular, a dining room was added on the tenth floor with a view of Lake Michigan. Also a banquet hall with additional 600 tons, located directly over the auditorium and supported by two iron trusses spanning almost 115 feet.

The relatively high ground-water level and the extra weight of the tower caused additional technical problems during construction. The total settlement of the ten-story building was expected to increase greatly after construction of the seventeen-story tower. In order to prevent uneven settlement, Adler decided to pre-stress the supporting soil before construction through an artificial loading of the foundation of the tower with its estimated overweight compared with the rest of the building. As the tower rose above the height of the adjacent wall of the building, the artificial load was decreased, by an amount equal to that of the portion of the completed building.

Acoustic ceiling panels were again used as the basis of the design of the auditorium. A normal concert held 4237 people. With mobile ceiling and floor sections, the seating capacity could be decreased to 2574 seats for recitals and

rium neben den technischen Innovationen auch der Tatsache, daß unter den rund 50 Zeichnern Frank Lloyd Wright ab 1888 als «the designing partner's ‹pencil› » arbeitete (Wright 1949, S. 53). War Adler für die physische Konstitution des Gebäudes maßgebend, so brachte es Sullivan «zum Singen» (Wright 1949, S. 95). Im Gegensatz zu den eher nüchternen Fassaden sind alle inneren Oberflächen «all-over» mit Mosaiken, Stukkaturen oder Wandmalereien bedeckt. Die Grundfarbe des Auditoriums ist elfenbeinern, die Stukkaturen sind in einem etwas dunkleren Ton gehalten oder golden bemalt. In den Stukkaturen der elliptischen Gurtbögen wurden eine große Anzahl von Edison-Glühbirnen sowie Lüftungsgitter integriert. Unter den beigezogenen Künstlern befanden sich zwei Franzosen, die zur selben Zeit wie Sullivan an der Beaux-Arts studiert hatten und nun am Art Institute of Chicago unterrichteten: Louis Millet war zuständig für die Schablonenmalerei an den Wänden, von Albert A. Fleury stammen die beiden Lünettenfresken «Frühling» und «Herbst» links und rechts im Saal auf der Höhe des ersten Balkons. Sie illustrieren zwei Passagen aus Sullivans Prosagedicht mit dem Titel «Inspiration», das der Autor 1886 den staunenden Architekten der Western Association vorgetragen hatte.

1888 wurde im noch unvollendeten Auditorium Benjamin Harrison zum republikanischen Präsidentschaftskandidaten nominiert. Er war auch ein Jahr später als 27. Präsident der Vereinigten Staaten anwesend, als das Auditorium offiziell eröffnet wurde. Adler & Sullivan richteten sich, äußeres Zeichen ihres Aufstiegs, im obersten Geschoß des Turmes ein, der damals das höchste Bauwerk Chicagos war. Finanziell gesehen erwies sich das «gargantueske» Bauwerk als ein eher zerbrechlich' Ding. Nur gerade 1893 konnten Dividenden ausbezahlt werden. 1908 stand das Unternehmen vor dem Ruin, und Sullivan zeichnete bereits an Plänen für einen Wolkenkratzer an Stelle des Auditoriums. 1928 machte das Auditorium schließlich bankrott, entging jedoch seiner Zerstörung einzig deshalb, weil die Abbruchkosten höher gewesen wären als der Preis für neues Bauland in vergleichbarer Lage. Während des Krieges wurde das Gebäude von der Armee in Beschlag genommen. Seit 1946 gehört es der Roosevelt University. Bühne und Saal dienen nach wie vor großen musikalischen Aufführungen.

increased for conventions to 7000. The size of the project alone necessitated pioneering innovations in acoustics, stage mechanics, ventilation, and energy use.

The importance of the auditorium in the history of modern architecture is due not only to the technical ingenuity of the architects but also to the fact that, among almost 50 draftsmen, Frank Lloyd Wright became "the designing partner's 'pencil'" in 1888. (Wright 1949, p. 53) If the physical aspects of the building were primarily Adler's responsibility, then Sullivan made it "sing". (Wright 1949, p. 95). In contrast to the rather sober exterior façades, the interior surfaces are covered with mosaics, plaster reliefs or murals. Although the main color of the auditorium is ivory, the plaster ornament is either in a darker tone or painted gold. The plaster reliefs decorating the expanding elliptical transverse arches were studded with numerous Edison-lights and ventilation grilles. Among the many artists involved in the project were two Frenchmen who had studied with Sullivan at the Beaux-Arts and were teaching at that time at the Art Institute of Chicago: Louis Millet decorated the walls with stencilled patterns and Albert A. Fleury did the two allegorical lunette frescoes, "Spring" and "Fall", placed at the same height as the dress circle, on the left and right side, respectively, of the auditorium. They illustrate two passages from Sullivan's prose-poetry entitled "Inspiration" which the author had presented before an astonished crowd at the convention of the Western Association of Architects in 1886.

In 1888, a year before its completion, Benjamin Harrison was nominated as the Republican presidential candidate in the auditorium. One year later, Harrison was again present at the official opening of the auditorium as the 27th President of the United States. As a sign of their success, Adler & Sullivan moved their offices into the top floor of the tower which at that time was the tallest building ever erected in Chicago. However, the "gargantuan" structure turned out to be a financial flop. Dividends could only be paid in 1893. In 1908 the building was on the verge of bankruptcy. Sullivan had already drawn up plans for a new skyscraper to be erected on the same site. The auditorium finally went bankrupt in 1928. It was saved from destruction only because the cost of tearing it down would have been higher than the price of commercial real estate in a comparable area. During the war, the building was taken over by the army. Since 1946 it has belonged to Roosevelt University. The auditorium is still used for large musical events.

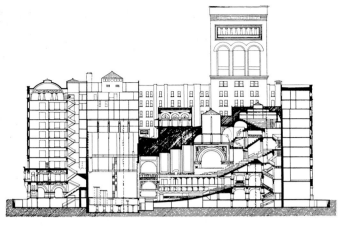

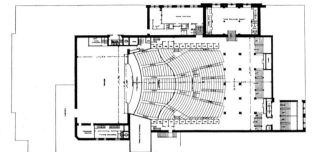

Grundriß des Erdgeschosses
und Längsschnitt.
*Main floor plan and
longitudinal section.*

Der Theatersaal, Photos von
Henry Fuermann.
*The Auditorium theatre,
Photos by Henry Fuermann.*

Die Bar und der große
Treppenaufgang im
Auditorium Hotel, Photos von
Henry Fuermann.
The bar and the big staircase
in the Auditorium hotel,
Photos by Henry Fuermann.

Linke Seite / *left page:*
Links: Dekoratives Muster im
Theatersaal.
Left: Stencil used in the
Auditorium theatre.

Rechts: Aus Ruprich-Roberts
Kurs «Composition
d'ornament» an der École
impériale et spéciale de dessin
in Paris, publiziert 1853.
Right: From Ruprich-Robert's
course «Composition of
ornament» at the École
impériale et spéciale de dessin
in Paris, published 1853.

Der Turm an der
Congress Street, Photo von
Richard Nickel.
The Auditorium tower
on Congress Street, Photo
by Richard Nickel.

Haus für den Standard Club 1887/88, Anbau 1892

Michigan Avenue und 24th Street, Chicago;
1931 abgerissen

Der Auftrag kam von der angesehensten jüdischen Organisation Chicagos, zu deren Gründungsmitgliedern im Jahre 1869 auch Geschäftsleute gehörten, die später verschiedentlich mit Adler & Sullivan zusammenarbeiteten (so u. a. Selz und Schwab). Wenn auch das bossierte Quadermauerwerk eindeutig auf Richardson zurückgeführt werden konnte, so war die asymmetrische Fassadenkomposition entlang der 24th Street völlig neuartig: Fenster wurden zu Kolossalöffnungen zusammengefaßt, oder sie lösten sich aus ihrem Verband und setzten sich in einer Reihe einzelner Elemente fort. 1892 wurden Adler & Sullivan mit einem südlichen Anbau beauftragt. Statt von richardsonesker Romanik war die Loggia zur Michigan Avenue hin von üppig dekorierter maurischer Architektur inspiriert. Diesen Anbau ersetzte Abraham K. Adler, der Sohn von Dankmar, der nach dem Tode seines Vaters mit Samuel A. Treat ein Architekturbüro führte, später durch einen neungeschossigen Baukörper und glich ihn der Formensprache der ersten Bauetappe an.

Standard Club House 1887/88, Addition 1892

Michigan Avenue and 24th Street, Chicago;
demolished in 1931

The Standard Club, the most respected Jewish organization in Chicago, founded in 1869, commissioned this building. Among the founding members were businessmen who collaborated with Adler & Sullivan on several occasions (including Selz and Schwab). Even though the rusticated ashlar masonry can undoubtedly be traced back to Richardson, the asymmetrical composition of the façade on 24th Street was completely new: the individual windows were united to form colossal openings or they were separated from the group to continue in a row of individual elements. In 1892 Adler & Sullivan were commissioned to do an addition on the south side of the building. However, instead of Richardsonian Romanesque, the loggia on Michigan Avenue was inspired by elaborately decorated moorish architecture. This addition was later replaced by a nine-floor structure that adhered to the formal articulation of the first phase of construction. Abraham K. Adler, son of Dankmar, who had opened an architectural office with his partner, Samuel A. Treat, designed this addition.

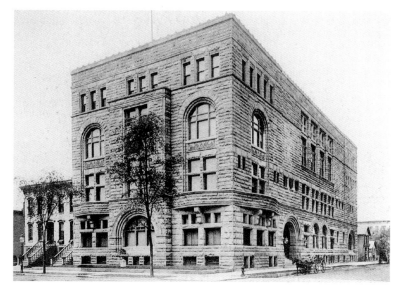

Straßenfassaden.
Street elevations.

Walker Warenhaus   1888/89

Ecke Adams und Market Streets, Chicago;
1953 abgerissen

Ursprünglich für Martin A. Ryerson geplant, wurde der
Bau dann vom Möbelhersteller James H. Walker bezogen.
Auch dieses Gebäude war dem romanesken Stil von
Richardsons berühmtem Bau für Marshall Fields ver-
pflichtet. Frank Lloyd Wright gegenüber soll sich Sulli-
van wie folgt über diesen Entwurf geäußert haben: «Wright, there is the last word in Romanesque.» (van
Zanten 1986, S. 36). Ein anderer Angestellter erinnert
sich an folgenden Kommentar von Sullivan: «I'm going to
show 'em in the Walker building more than Richardson
ever knew». Diese Worte weisen darauf hin, daß die Va-
riationen an den formalen Anleihen bei Richardson von
großer Bedeutung sind, insbesondere die glatten Fassadenoberflächen und die großen Rundbogen mit mehrfach
abgetrepptem Gewände. Man kann darin eine weitere
Reduktion des architektonischen Vokabulars sehen, so
daß das Bauwerk wie eine rein «abstrakte Komposition»
(Morrison 1935, S. 115) wirkte.

Walker Warehouse   1888/89

Corner Adams and Market Streets, Chicago;
demolished in 1953

Although originally designed for Martin A. Ryerson, the
warehouse was actually occupied by the furniture-maker
James H. Walker. The general design concept was inspired by the Romanesque Revival style of Richardson's
famous Marshall Field Building. Apparently Sullivan told
Frank Lloyd Wright the following about this design:
"Wright, there is the last word in Romanesque." (van
Zanten 1986, p. 36) Another employee remembers Sullivan remarking: "I'm going to show 'em in the Walker
building more than Richardson ever knew". These comments reveal that the differences in the formal treatment
of Richardson's influence are significant, particularly the
smooth surfaces of the façade devoid of any ornament
and the large round arches whose jambs are recessed in
successive steps from the wall plane. Sullivan reduces
the architectonic vocabulary even further, so that the
structure has the over-all effect of a purely "abstract composition" (Morrison 1935, p. 115).

Photo von Henry Fuermann.
Photo by Henry Fuermann.

Kehilath Anshe Ma'ariv Synagogue   1889/90

Ecke 33rd Street und Indiana Avenue, Chicago
Abraham Kohn, der Schwiegervater von Dankmar Adler, gründete diese jüdische Gemeinde im Jahre 1861. Er berief damals Dankmars Vater als Rabbi nach Chicago. Entsprechend einem ersten Entwurf von Adler & Sullivan hätten die Mauern der Synagoge aus glatten Quadersteinen steil geböscht aufsteigen sollen. Aus Kostengründen mußte jedoch auf bossierte Sandsteine für den unteren und gepreßte Metallplatten für den oberen Teil der Fassade zurückgegriffen werden. Jeder einzelne Fensterflügel erscheint wie aus der Fassadenfläche herausgestanzt und ergibt zusammen mit benachbarten eine Art Kolossalordnung der Öffnungen. Der große Versammlungssaal befindet sich im ersten Obergeschoß und ist nach akustischen Prinzipien gestaltet. Reiche Dekorationen finden sich in Bandform an der Brüstung der Galerie, an den Gurtbögen der Decke und unmittelbar unter dem Ansatz des Lichtgadens. Das Muldengewölbe ist mit Eichenholz getäfert und füllt den ganzen Lichtgaden aus.

Kehilath Anshe Ma'ariv Synagogue   1889/90

Corner 33rd Street and Indiana Avenue, Chicago
Abraham Kohn, Adler's father-in-law and founder of the Anshe Ma'ariv Congregation (1861), appointed Dankmar's father, Liebman Adler, to become its first rabbi. According to a preliminary design by Adler & Sullivan, the walls of the synagogue were to be battered and constructed entirely out of smooth ashlar blocks. Instead they were forced to resort to a cheaper rough-hewn sandstone for the lower portion of the façade and pressed sheet metal for the upper section to reduce costs. Each individual window looks cut out of the plane of the façade; when combined whith adjacent windows, they form a colossal order of openings. The design of the large congregation hall on the second floor was determined by acoustic principles. Richly decorated bands of terra-cotta face the balustrade of the gallery, the transverse ribs on the ceiling, and the base of the clerestory. The vault is lined with oak panels and fills the clerestory.

Kultraum im Obergeschoß, Photo von Henry Fuermann.
The assembly hall on the 2nd floor, Photo by Henry Fuermann.

Erster Entwurf Sullivans.
Preliminary design by Sullivan.

Photo von Richard Nickel.
Photo by Richard Nickel.

Opera House Block 1889/90

Pueblo, Colorado; 1922 durch Feuer zerstört

Der Turm, die Dachloggia, das weit auskragende Walmdach und das rustizierte Mauerwerk ließen das Opernhaus von Pueblo, einer Kleinstadt im Westen der USA mit damals rund fünfundzwanzigtausend Einwohnern, wie einen florentinischen Renaissancepalast erscheinen (Morrison 1935, S. 118). Anläßlich seiner Italienreise hatte sich Sullivan immerhin sechs Wochen in Florenz aufgehalten. Das Theater mit einem Fassungsvermögen von nahezu 1000 Personen war von kommerziellen Nutzungen, unter anderem einer Bank, umgeben. Erstmals wurden hier die verschiedenen Eingänge entsprechend ihrer Bedeutung mit reich verzierten Rahmen ausgezeichnet, die vor der eigentlichen Fassadenflucht lagen. Im Grundriß bildete der Zuschauerraum ein Rechteck, in das durch Logen und Balkone ein Achteck eingeschrieben war. Die Form der Decke allerdings folgte nicht der Logik eines Zentralraums, sondern schwang sich von der Bühne ausgehend stufenweise hoch bis über die letzten Zuschauerränge.

Opera House Block 1889/90

Pueblo, Colorado; destroyed by fire in 1922

This opera house was erected in Pueblo, a small town in the western United States which then had a population of nearly 25 000. The tower, the roof-loggia, the hipped roof, the large projecting cornice, and the rusticated masonry gave the Opera House the appearance of a Florentine Renaissance palace (Morrison 1935, p. 118). (While traveling in Italy, Sullivan did spend six weeks in Florence.) The theater, with a seating capacity of nearly 1000 people, was enclosed by offices, a bank, etc. This was the first time that ornately decorated frames projecting from the actual plane of the façade were used to distinguish various entrances according to their function. On the floor plan, the auditorium forms a square in which an octagan is inscribed by the arrangement of the boxes and balconies. The shape of the ceiling, however, does not follow the logic of a central space; instead it sweeps up from the stage all the way over the last row of seats.

Grundriß des Erdgeschosses und Schnitt.
Main floor plan and section.

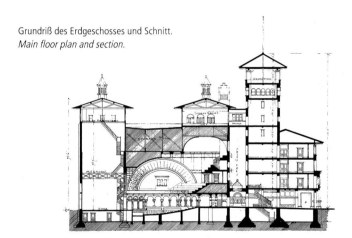

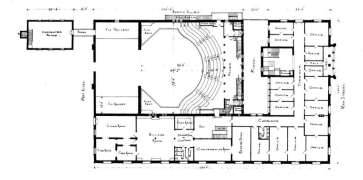

80

Theatersaal mit Blick zum Zuschauerraum, Zeichnung.
The interior of the theatre with view to the auditorium, drawing.

Straßenfassaden.
Street elevations.

Ferienhäuser für Helen und James Charnley sowie für Louis H. Sullivan   1890

Ocean Springs, Mississippi

In Begleitung des Ehepaars Charnley kam Sullivan im Winter 1889/90 nach Ocean Springs (Mississippi), um sich vom beruflichen Streß zu erholen. Der kleine Ort am Golf von Mexiko wurde von wohlhabenden Einwohnern Chicagos vorzugsweise als Winterquartier aufgesucht. Während des darauffolgenden Sommers entstanden die beiden Ferienhäuser mit zugehörigen Nebenbauten auf benachbarten Grundstücken. Sullivan schätzte diesen Ort als Quelle für Inspirationen und Entspannung: Er widmete sich leidenschaftlich der Anlage des Gartens und der Rosenzucht. Die Horizontalität der Bauten mit den großen Loggien auf den Vorderseiten nehmen Stilmerkmale der späteren «Prairie School Architecture» vorweg. Ob die Bauten deshalb tatsächlich Frank Lloyd Wright zugeschrieben werden müssen, wie dieser beanspruchte, bleibt angesichts von Sullivans gefühlsmäßiger Bindung an den Ort, den Wright nie gesehen hat, fraglich.

Vacation Cottages for Helen and James Charnley and for Louis H. Sullivan   1890

Ocean Springs, Mississippi

Sullivan accompanied the Charnleys to Ocean Springs, Mississippi during the winter of 1889/90 to relax from the rigors and stress of the office. This small town on the Gulf of Mexico was the most popular winter resort for well-to-do Chicagoans. Both of these summer cottages with their adjoining buildings were erected on adjacent lots the following summer. The place became a great source of inspiration and relaxation for Sullivan: he was passionately devoted to planting a garden and cultivating roses. The horizontality of the structures with large loggias on the front sides of the building anticipate stylistic features of the later "Prairie School Architecture". Whether or not this justifies ascribing these buildings to Frank Lloyd Wright, as Wright claimed, remains questionable, especially considering Sullivan's emotional bond to this place which Wright himself had never visited.

Ein Rosenbusch – Symbol für Sullivans Verbundenheit mit dem Ort: Abbildung aus Architectural Record, 1905.
A rose bush – symbol of Sullivan's care for the site: illustration out of Architectural Record, 1905.

Lageplan von Sullivans Grundstück.
Siteplan of the Sullivan property.

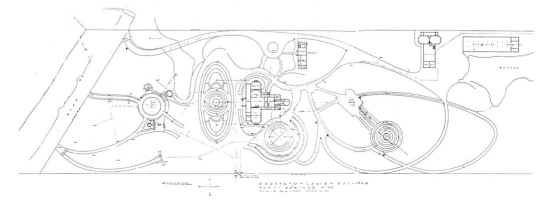

Wasserturm des Hauses
Sullivan.
*Water tower of Sullivan's
cottage.*

Haus Sullivan,
Photo von Henry Fuermann.
*The Sullivan cottage,
Photo by Henry Fuermann.*

Ontario Hotel   1890 (Projekt);
Dooly Block   1890/91

111 West 2nd South Street, Salt Lake City, Utah

Zwei der insgesamt vier Aufträge, die Adler & Sullivan aus dem Westen der USA erhielten, betrafen Projekte in Salt Lake City. Mit den Fundamenten für das Hotel Ontario wurde im November 1890 begonnen, bevor die Arbeiten aus unbekannten Gründen für immer eingestellt wurden. Wie beim Opernhaus von Pueblo zeigten sich in diesem Projekt erneut Elemente italienischer Renaissance-Palazzi.

Der zweite Auftrag in Salt Lake City betraf ein Geschäftshaus auf einem angrenzenden Grundstück. Im Werk von Adler & Sullivan markiert der Dooly Block den Übergang zu einer neuen Gestaltungsweise: er ist der glatten und schmucklosen Fassadenoberflächen wegen dem Walker Warehouse verwandt, doch die Komposition der Öffnungen nimmt bereits Wolkenkratzer wie das Union Trust Building in St. Louis oder das Schiller Building in Chicago vorweg. Schließlich findet sich im weit auskragenden, schweren Dachgesimse, das mit einem Terrakotta-Fries von ineinandergeschobenen Ringen verziert ist, eine Entsprechung zum gleichzeitigen Wainwright Building in St. Louis.

Ontario Hotel   1890 (Project);
Dooly Block   1890/91

111 West 2nd South Street, Salt Lake City, Utah

Two of a total of four commissions which Adler & Sullivan received in the western United States were projects in Salt Lake City. However, construction of the Hotel Ontario was terminated indefinitely for unknown reasons, just after construction of the foundations had begun in November 1890. As in the Pueblo Opera House, elements of Italian Renaissance Palazzi were also evident here.

Their second commission in Salt Lake City was an office building on an adjacent lot. The Dooly Block marks the transition to a new style in the work of Adler & Sullivan: due to the smooth and unadorned surface of the façade, this structure is clearly allied to the Walker Warehouse, although the arrangement of openings foreshadows skyscrapers like the Union Trust Building in St. Louis or the Schiller Building in Chicago. In addition, the heavy projecting cornice faced with a decorative terra-cotta frieze of interlocking rings is a feature which corresponds to the Wainwright Building erected at the same time in St. Louis.

Links Ontario Hotel (nicht ausgeführt), rechts Dooly Block.
Left the Ontario Hotel (not executed), right the Dooly Block.

Grabmal für Carrie Elizabeth Getty   1890
Graceland Cemetery, Chicago
Das Grabmal liegt nicht weit von jenem für Martin A.
Ryerson entfernt. Von den «Fesseln der Funktionalität»
befreit, konnte sich Sullivan in diesem Falle der Architektur als rein künstlerischer Disziplin widmen. Zwischen der
vorspringenden Bodenplatte und der auskragenden
Dachplatte besteht der Baukörper aus zwei deutlich
unterschiedenen Teilen: der untere ist aus glatt poliertem
Sandstein, während der obere etwas zurückversetzt und
mit einem geometrischen Muster überzogen ist. Auf jeder
Seite greift ein aus glatten Quadern gefügter Bogen in
den oberen Teil hinein. Die geometrischen Muster unter-
brechen den tektonischen Aufbau, so daß die schwere
Dachplatte über den Bögen zu schweben scheint. Beispiele einer solchen formalen Gliederung hatte Sullivan in
Paris an Bauten seines Lehrers Emile Vaudremer beobachten können.

Tomb for Carrie Elizabeth Getty   1890
Graceland Cemetery, Chicago
The Getty tomb is sited near the tomb of Martin A. Ryerson. Freed here from the "chains of functionality", Sullivan could finally devote himself to architecture as a pure
artistic discipline. The main structure between the projecting ground slab and the overhanging roof slab is a rect-
angular block with two distinctly different sections: the
lower half is of smoothly polished sandstone, while the
upper half is slightly recessed and covered with an incised
geometric pattern. On each side an arch composed of
smooth wedge-shaped voussoirs projects into the upper
section of the cube. The geometric patterns interrupt the
tectonic structure, so that the heavy roof slab above the
arches seems to be weightless. Sullivan was exposed to
examples of this kind of formal composition in buildings
of his teacher Emile Vaudremer in Paris.

Photo von Henry Fuermann.
Photo by Henry Fuermann.

Wainwright Building   1890–1892

Nordwestecke 7th und Chestnut Streets, St. Louis

Der erste wirkliche Wolkenkratzer von Adler & Sullivan entstand im Auftrag des Biermagnaten Ellis Wainwright und seiner Mutter Catherine. Seine Tragstruktur beruht vollständig auf einem feuersicher verkleideten Eisenskelett, eine Konstruktionsweise, die William Le Baron Jenney mit dem Home Insurance Building (1883–1885) für Geschäftshochhäuser eingeführt hatte. Frank Lloyd Wright beschreibt den Entwurf als Resultat eines plötzlichen Einfalls, den Sullivan in «literally three minutes» skizziert hatte. «This was Louis Sullivan's greatest moment – his greatest effort. The ‹skyscraper› as a new thing beneath the sun, an entity with virtue, individuality and beauty all its own, was born» (Wright 1924, S. 29). So verstanden auch zeitgenössische Kritiker das Wainwright Building als Durchbruch in der Gestaltung von Hochhäusern mit tragendem Eisenskelett. Doch die Komposition der Fassade läßt sich nicht unmittelbar aus der Konstruktionsweise ableiten – weder die Betonung des Volumens als Ganzes noch die der Eckpfeiler stimmt mit den konstruktiven Gegebenheiten überein. Zudem wurden alle vertikalen Streben gleich ausgebildet, obwohl sich nur hinter jeder zweiten eine Eisenstütze befindet. Philipp Johnson folgerte aus dieser Differenz zwischen Konstruktion und Fassade: «Sullivan's interest was not in structure, but design» (Johnson 1956).

In diesem Sinne haben auch Frank Lloyd Wright und Hugh Morrison, der die wohl immer noch beste Monographie über Sullivan verfaßt hat, den zutiefst klassischen Charakter des Wainwright Buildings unterstrichen: «Base, shaft and capital were there with no direct or apparent relation to actual construction» (Wright 1949, S. 75). Was trotzdem die spezifische architekturhistorische Bedeutung des Wainwright Buildings für die Moderne ausmacht, läßt sich mit einem Vergleich zum Zweiten Leiter Building (1889–1891) von Le Baron Jenney darlegen. Bezüglich der Konstruktion stimmen beide Bauten in der Anwendung neuster Errungenschaften überein. In beiden Fällen werden auch die Umrisse der Bauvolumen betont. Doch während die mittlere Fassadenpartie des Leiter Building durch hierarchisch aufgebaute Systeme von Pfeilern und Balken weiter unterteilt wurde, ergeben die horizontalen und vertikalen Streifen des Wainwright Building ein gleichförmiges Netz, das die Zellstruktur der Büros zum Ausdruck bringt.

Wainwright Building   1890–1892

Northwest corner of 7th and Chestnut Streets, St. Louis

Thanks to a commission from the brewing magnate Ellis Wainwright and his mother Catherine, Adler & Sullivan built their first true skyscraper. Its load-bearing construction entirely consists of a steel frame encased in fireproof tile – a method of construction introduced for tall office buildings by William Le Baron Jenney with the Home Insurance Building (1883–1885). Frank Lloyd Wright describes the design as a sudden impulse that Sullivan had sketched in "literally three minutes". "This was Louis Sullivan's greatest moment – his greatest effort. The 'skyscraper' as a new thing beneath the sun, an entity with virtue, individuality and beauty all its own, was born." (Wright 1924, p. 29) Similarly, contemporary critics claimed that the Wainwright Building was a breakthrough in the design of multi-story buildings with a load-bearing steel frame. Yet the design of the façade can not be immediately derived from the method of construction – neither the emphasis on the volume as a whole, nor on the corner piers reveals the actual structural facts of the building. In addition, all the vertical piers are treated with equal emphasis, even though there is a steel column only behind each second pier (false piers). From the discrepancy between structure and façade, Philip Johnson concluded: "Sullivan's interest was not in structure, but design" (Johnson, 1956).

Accordingly, Frank Lloyd Wright and Hugh Morrison, who has still written probably the best monograph ever about Sullivan, have both pointed out the underlying classical character of the Wainwright Building: "Base, shaft and capital were there with no direct or apparent relation to actual construction." (Wright 1949, p. 75) Nevertheless, the specific significance of the Wainwright Building for modern architecture can be elucidated by comparing it to the Second Leiter Building of Le Baron Jenney (1889–1891). In terms of construction, both edifices are the same in the application of the newest technical innovations (use of metal-skeleton construction). In both cases, the outline of the volume of the building is emphasized. However, while the central section of the façade of the Leiter Building was subdivided further by a hierarchical arrangement of piers and beams, the horizontal and vertical lines (pier and spandrel) of the Wainwright Building create a uniform grid that expresses the cell structure of the individual offices.

William Le Baron Jenney:
Zweites Leiter Building,
Chicago, 1889–1891.
William Le Baron Jenney:
Second Leiter Building,
Chicago, 1889–1891.

Wainwright Building während
der Bauarbeiten.
Wainwright Building under
construction.

Ansicht und Details der Fassade.
General view and details of the elevation.

Typischer Grundriß des 3.–9. Geschosses.
Typical plan of 3rd–9th floor.

Schiller Building   1890–1892

64 West Randolph Street, Chicago; 1961 abgerissen
Wegen zahlreicher Änderungen am Bauprogramm zog
sich die Entwurfsphase über ein Jahr hin. Ende 1892
konnten das Theater mit 1270 Sitzplätzen, die verschiedenen Räume der German Opera Company sowie 342
Büros bezogen werden. Es handelte sich um das höchste
je von Adler & Sullivan realisierte Gebäude. In derselben
Zeit und auf Grund der gleichen konstruktiven Voraussetzungen wie das Wainwright Building konzipiert, wich die
Gestalt des Schiller Building erheblich von diesem ab. Aus
Rücksicht auf benachbarte Bauten, aber auch zum Vorteil
der Belichtung der im hinteren Teil gelegenen Büros,
wurde das Bauvolumen in einzelne, gestaffelte Teile gegliedert und jeder mit besonders dekorierten Elementen
(Erker, Loggien, Dachgesimse) ausgezeichnet. Im Zuschauerraum wurden Bögen und Gewölbeschalen tele-
skopartig vom Proszenium der Bühne aus entwickelt. In
diesem letzten Theatersaal von Adler & Sullivan glückte
den Architekten eine «meisterhafte Orchestrierung» (van
Zanten 1986, S. 48) aller technischen und dekorativen
Mittel.

Schiller Building   1890–1892

64 West Randolph Street, Chicago; demolished in 1961
Due to numerous changes in the building plan, the design
phase was prolonged over a whole year. Finally, late in
1892 the building was completed. It contained a theater
with 1270 seats, various rooms of the German Opera
Company as well as 342 offices. This was the tallest building Adler & Sullivan ever actually built. Although constructed at the same time and with the same structural
requirements as the Wainwright Building, the exterior of
the Schiller Building differs considerably from the Wainwright. Out of consideration for the adjacent buildings
and to obtain necessary light to the offices in the back, the
set-back system was employed: the building consisted of
blocks of varying height, each distinctively decorated with
individual elements (bay windows, loggias, cornices). The
ceiling of the auditorium consisted of a series of expanding semi-circular arches and segmental vaults which were
extended like a telescope from the proscenium to the balcony. In this last auditorium of Adler & Sullivan, the architects succeeded in a "masterful orchestration" (van
Zanten 1986, p. 48) of all technical and decorative
means.

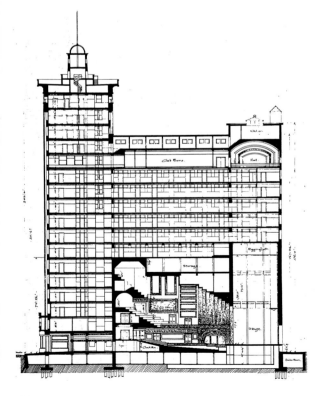

Projekt für einen Leuchtturm von G. André, École des
Beaux-Arts 1870, publiziert 1877 (Ausschnitt).
*Lighthouse project by G. André, École des Beaux-Arts
1870, published 1877 (detail).*

Längsschnitt.
Longitudinal section.

Rechte Seite / *right page*:
Schiller Building mit Borden Block im Vordergrund,
Photo von Henry Fuermann.
*Schiller Building with Borden Block in the
foreground, photo by Henry Fuermann.*

Grundriß des Erdgeschosses.
First floor plan.

Bühnenportal,
Photo von Richard Nickel.
Proscenium,
Photo by Richard Nickel.

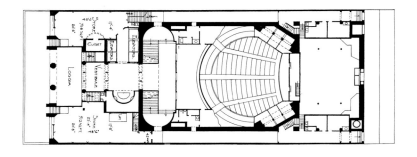

Grundrisse des 15. und 17. Geschosses.
Plans of the 15th and 17th floor.

Bühnenraum, Photo von Richard Nickel.
Stage, photo by Richard Nickel.

Transportation Building   1891–1893

World's Columbian Exposition, Chicago; abgerissen

Für den Bau der Weltausstellung von 1893 in Chicago forderte der verantwortliche Direktor, Daniel H. Burnham, im Dezember 1890 zehn führende Architekturbüros zur Teilnahme auf. Dabei handelte es sich außer Adler & Sullivan um die Büros von Cobb, Jenney, Frost und Burling & Whitehouse, alle in Chicago ansässig, und um die Büros von Hunt, Post, McKim Mead & White und Peabody & Stearns, Waren & Van Brunt, die alle von der Ostküste stammten. Adler & Sullivan waren bereit, das Ausstellungsgebäude des Verkehrswesens zu übernehmen. Die einzige verbindliche Rahmenbedingung bestand in der Traufhöhe von 19,5 Metern. Konstruktions- und Werkpläne wurden vom Baubüro der Ausstellung ausgearbeitet.

Das Transportation Building mit seinem «Golden Doorway» wurde zum Publikumsliebling unter all den vornehmen weißen Interpretationen klassischer Architektur. Zudem fand erstmals ein Entwurf Sullivans auch internationale Beachtung: die «Société Centrale des Arts Decoratifs» in Paris zeichnete das Transportation Building als einziges Bauwerk der ganzen Weltausstellung mit einer Medaille aus. Was schon wegen der Trennung zwischen Entwurfs- und Konstruktionsbüro nahelag, unterstrich Sullivan in einer programmatischen Erklärung zu seinen Absichten. In einem Brief vom 11. November 1893 an den Direktor heißt es: «In designing the Transportation Building, its architects sought to illustrate the elementary processes of architectural composition. They wished to do this independently of the notion of style as the word is usually understood; and yet to seek for style as they understand it, namely, as a quality due to a certain way of expressing the development of an idea. We have sought to demonstrate in our work, that the word style really implies first a *harmonious system of thinking,* second, an equally *harmonious manner of expressing the thought.*» Der konkrete Zweck des Ausstellungsgebäudes diente nur als Vorwand, um Prinzipien der architektonischen Dekoration zu behandeln. Es handelte sich nicht um Architektur im eigentlichen Sinne, sondern um ein «picture-building» (Wright 1924, S. 29) oder um ein im großen Maßstab realisiertes «System of Architectural Ornament», wie der Titel der letzten Publikation Sullivans heißt. Nicht zufällig auch glich der «Golden Doorway» dem dekorativ gestalteten Bühnentrichter des Schiller-Theaters.

Sullivan zufolge hatte die Weltausstellung insgesamt

Transportation Building   1891–1893

World's Columbian Exposition, Chicago; demolished

The director in charge of the construction of the 1893 World's Fair in Chicago, Daniel H. Burnham, asked ten leading architectural firms to participate in December, 1890. Adler & Sullivan were among the many firms represented at the Fair: Cobb, Jenney, Frost and Burling & Whitehouse were all from Chicago; the offices of Hunt, Post, McKim Mead & White, Peabody & Stearns, and Waren & Van Brunt were East-Coast based. After initial negotiations, Adler & Sullivan were ready to take on the Transportation Building. The only binding condition on the project for all the buildings was the pre-determined height of 65 feet for the main cornice. Construction and work plans were organized by the Department of Construction of the Fair.

Among the predominantly elegant "chaste white" interpretations of classical architecture at the Fair, the Transportation Building with its "Golden Doorway" became the most popular building for visitors. Moreover, this was the first design of Sullivan's to receive international recognition: the "Société Centrale des Arts Décoratifs" in Paris honored the Transportation Building by selecting it as the only structure in the Fair to receive a medal. What was already obvious, due to the division between architect and engineer, was substantiated by Sullivan in a programmatic statement concerning his intentions. In a letter dated November 11, 1893 to Burnham, he stated: "In designing the Transportation Building, its architects sought to illustrate the elementary processes of architectural composition. They wished to do this independently of the notion of style as the word is usually understood; and yet to seek for style as they understand it, namely, as a quality due to a certain way of expressing the development of an idea. We have sought to demonstrate in our work, that the word style really implies first a *harmonious system of thinking*, second, an equally *harmonious manner of expressing the thought.*" The concrete purpose of the exposition building, then, served only as a pretext for the expression of certain principles of architectonic ornament. It is not concerned with architecture *per se,* but with "picture-building" (Wright 1924, p. 29) or with a large-scale realization of a "System of Architectural Ornament", incidentally the title of Sullivan's last publication. It is not a coincidence that the "Golden Doorway" resembled the decoratively designed funnel-shaped stage of the Schiller Theater.

verheerende Auswirkungen auf die Entwicklung einer amerikanischen Architektur. Er schreibt in seiner Autobiographie von einer langandauernden, kulturellen Verdunkelung, die durch die klassizistischen Stilimitationen der Ausstellung verursacht wurde.

According to Sullivan, the World's Fair had a disastrous effect on the development of a specifically American architecture. He writes about a lasting cultural darkening caused by the classicist style imitations of the Fair.

Gebäude der Chicagoer Weltausstellung von 1893, von oben: Transportation Building von Adler & Sullivan; Horticultural Building von W. L. B. Jenney; Fine Arts Building von C. B. Atwood; Machinery Building von Peabody & Stearns.

Pavillions of the World's Columbia Exposition 1893, from above: Transportation Building, Adler & Sullivan architects; Horticultural Building by W. L. B. Jenney; Fine Arts Building by C. B. Atwood; Machinery Building by Peabody & Stearns.

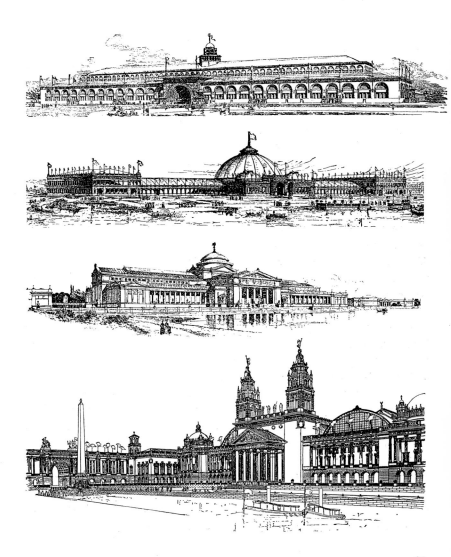

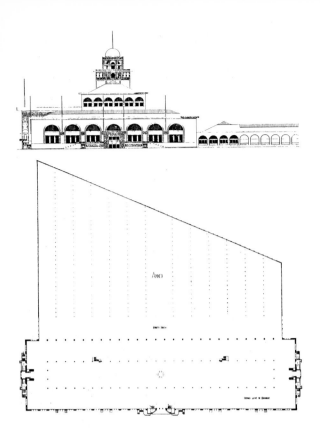

Ausstellungshalle, Photo von C. D. Arnold.
Interior, photo by C. D. Arnold.

Das «Goldene Tor», Photo von Henry Fuermann.
The «Golden Doorway», Photo by Henry Fuermann.

Haus Charnley   1891/92

1365 Astor Street, Chicago

Die Charnleys beauftragten Adler & Sullivan nach der Fertigstellung des Ferienhauses in Ocean Springs auch mit der Planung ihres Stadthauses in Chicago. Der Entwurf wird allgemein Frank Lloyd Wright zugeschrieben, aufgrund seiner Aussagen sowie auch gestützt durch die Tatsache, daß die großen Aufträge den beiden Partnern der Firma nicht viel Zeit für kleinere Projekte gelassen haben. Als weiteres Argument für diese Zuschreibung dient die Beobachtung, daß sich das Charnley-Haus wesentlich von früheren Wohnbauten von Adler & Sullivan abhebt. Allerdings unterscheidet es sich ebenso von Wohnbauten, die Wright zu jener Zeit unter eigenem oder fremdem Namen baute. Elemente wie die weit auskragende und verzierte Dachplatte, der reich ornamentierte Balkon sowie die «mariage des formes» von Sockel und Rahmung des Portals muten schließlich eher sullivanesk an.

Charnley Residence   1891/92

1365 Astor Street, Chicago

After completing their vacation cottage in Ocean Springs, the Charnleys commissioned Adler & Sullivan for their city residence in Chicago. The design is generally ascribed to Frank Lloyd Wright, according to him as well as because the large commissions were so time-consuming that neither partner had much time left for smaller projects. A further argument for attributing the design to Wright is stylistic. The Charnley residence differs considerably from the earlier residential architecture of Adler & Sullivan. However, it differs just as much from residential buildings that Wright designed at that time under his own name or an alias. Elements such as the large projecting roof slab with ornamental decoration, the richly ornate balcony as well as the "marriage of forms" of base and frame surrounding the portal are indeed more Sullivanesque.

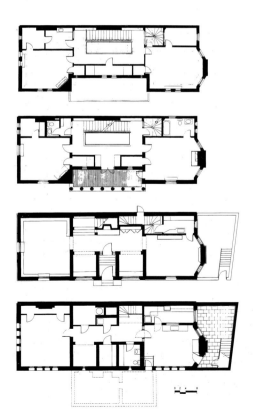

Grundrisse, Zeichnungen von Skidmore Owings & Merrill (SOM).
Floor plans, drawings by Skidmore Owings & Merrill (SOM).

Rechte Seite / *right page*:
Photo von Henry Fuermann.
Photo by Henry Fuermann.

Treppenhaus, Photo von Hedrich-Blessing.
Staircase, photo by Hedrich-Blessing.

Odd Fellows (Fraternity) Temple Building   1891

Chicago, Projekt

Das Projekt entstand im Auftrag der «Bruderschaft des Unabhängigen Ordens der Überzähligen», einer Art Freimaurerloge. Der vorgesehene Standort im Zentrum Chicagos blieb geheim, um Bodenspekulationen zu verhindern. Nur das 3.–6. und das 10. Geschoß sollten von der Bruderschaft belegt werden, während insgesamt 1100 Büros hätten vermietet werden können. Mit 36 Geschossen und einer Höhe von 137 Metern wäre dieses Gebäude für lange Zeit das höchste in Chicago gewesen. Seine Gestalt ergab sich aus der Bündelung unterschiedlich hoher Wainwright Buildings um einen mittleren Schaft. Die Abtreppung sollte die Gebäudehöhe akzeptierbar machen und nahm insofern das entscheidende Motiv des Zonierungsgesetzes von New York aus dem Jahre 1916 vorweg. Die Realisierung des Projekts scheiterte schließlich an der gesetzlichen Beschränkung der Bauhöhe.

In «The High Building Question», einem Artikel, der Ende 1891 in der Zeitschrift «The Graphic» publiziert wurde, entwickelte Sullivan eine Stadtvision mit Wolkenkratzern, jeder einen ganzen Straßenblock einnehmend, stufenweise abgetreppt und individuell bekrönt mit Zinnenkranz, Kuppel oder im Stile des Turmes des Auditorium Building.

Odd Fellows (Fraternity) Temple Building   1891

Chicago; project

This project was commissioned by "The Fraternity Association of the Independent Order of Odd Fellows", a type of Freemason society. In order to prevent land speculation, the site in the heart of downtown Chicago was kept secret. The fraternity rooms were to be located only on the third to the sixth and the tenth stories, while the remainder of the building containing a total of 1100 offices was available for rent. Its design resembled a cluster of Wainwright Buildings of varying heights placed around a central shaft. This system of set-backs, employed to make the height of the building more acceptable, anticipated the decisive reason for passing the New York Zoning Law of 1916. With 36 stories and a height of 450 feet, this proposed building would have been by far the largest and highest skyscraper ever built in Chicago for a long time. Nevertheless, the project was never realized because of a law restricting building height.

In an article entitled "The High Building Question", published in the magazine "The Graphic" in 1891, Sullivan developed a vision of the city of the future with set-back skyscrapers of staggered heights encompassing an entire city block, each building individually capped with a battlemented parapet, cupola or a tower in the style of the Auditorium Building.

Illustrationen zu Sullivans Artikel «The High Building Question» (1891).
Illustrations to Sullivan's essay on «The High Building Question» (1891).

Haus Sullivan   1891/92

4575 Lake Park Avenue, Chicago; 1970 abgerissen
Die Brüder Albert und Louis Sullivan planten das Wohnhaus in Chicago für ihre Mutter, die es jedoch nicht mehr
zu sehen bekam, da sie im Mai 1892 starb. Bis 1896
wurde es von Louis bewohnt, danach zog Albert mit seiner Familie ein. Der einfache Baukörper wurde an Dachgesims und Erker mit geometrischen, über dem Eingang
mit üppig floralen Ornamenten verziert. Ebenso wie die
Ferienhäuser in Ocean Springs und das Charnley-Haus in
Chicago wird auch dieses Wohnhaus von William A. Storer, in seinem vollständigen Werkkatalog zu Frank Lloyd
Wright, als Entwurf von Wright bezeichnet, jedoch als im
Stil des «lieben Meisters» ausgeführt (wie Wright Sullivan
nannte).

Sullivan Residence   1891/92

4575 Lake Park Avenue, Chicago; demolished in 1970
The brothers, Albert and Louis Sullivan, planned the residence in Chicago for their mother. She died in May 1892
before ever seeing it. Louis lived in the house until 1896,
after which it was occupied by Albert and his family. The
design of the building consisted of a simple block decorated with geometrically carved terra-cotta tiles on the
cornice and the bay window and an ornately carved floral
pattern on the semi-circular lunette over the entrance. In
his complete catalog of the work of Frank Lloyd Wright,
William A. Storer considers this residence, along with the
vacation cottages in Ocean Springs and the Charnley
house in Chicago, to be a design of Wright's, although
executed in the style of "der liebe Meister" (as Wright
named Sullivan).

Photo von Henry Fuermann.
Photo by Henry Fuermann.

Lünette aus Sandstein über dem Eingang.
Lunette of limestone above the entrance.

Brunswick-Balke-Collender-Fabrik   1881–1883, 1891

Superior, Huron, Orleans und Sedgwick Streets, Chicago; 1989 abgebrannt

John M. Brunswick, der 1834 aus der Schweiz nach Amerika ausgewandert war, hatte als Spezialist für Holzeinrichtungen in den siebziger Jahren großen Erfolg mit Billardtischen und fusionierte sein Geschäft mit jenen seiner wichtigsten Konkurrenten Balke (1873) und Collender (1884). Adler wurde bereits für die ersten Etappen der Fabrikanlage in den Jahren 1881, 1882 und 1883 engagiert. 1891 erhielten Adler & Sullivan den Auftrag, einen weiteren Teil innerhalb des Straßenblocks neu zu bebauen. Sie hielten sich weitgehend an die Formensprache des Trakts (B) von 1882, bestehend aus Backsteinfassaden von monumentaler Einfachheit. Der einzige plastische Schmuck bestand im Dachgesims, das wie ein reduzierter Wehrgang mit versetzt auskragenden Backsteinen gestaltet war. 1902 beauftragte Brunswick nicht Sullivan, sondern den Sohn des verstorbenen Dankmar Adler, Abraham K. Adler, mit der letzten Erweiterung der Fabrik.

Brunswick Balke Collender Factory   1881–1883, 1891

Superior, Huron, Orleans and Sedgwick Streets, Chicago; burned down in 1989

John M. Brunswick was a woodworking specialist emigrated from Switzerland to America in 1834, whose great success with billiard tables in the 1870s led him to merge with his biggest competitors, Balke (1873) and Collender (1884). Adler had already been commissioned for the first phases of construction of the factory complex in 1881, 1882 and 1883. In 1891 Adler & Sullivan were commissioned to design a new section within the city block. Formally, they adhered to the style of the block of 1882 which consisted of brick façades of monumental simplicity. The only sculptural ornament was the cornice treated as a reduced battlemented parapet with recessed projecting bricks. In 1902 Brunswick commissioned the son of the late Dankmar Adler, Abraham K. Adler, not Sullivan, for the final extension of the factory.

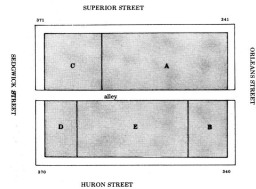

Lageplan: Bauten von Adler 1881 (A) und 1882 (B); Bauten von Adler & Sullivan 1891 (C) und 1893 (D); Erweiterung durch Abraham K. Adler 1902 (E).
Site plan: buildings by Adler 1881 (A) and 1882 (B); buildings by Adler & Sullivan 1891 (C) and 1893 (D); additions by Abraham K. Adler 1902 (E).

Zeichnung der Fassade an der Superior Street, 1891.
Drawing of the Superior Street elevation, 1891.

Ansicht des Gebäudes Ecke Superior/Sedgwick Streets.
Superior/Sedgwick Streets corner of the building.

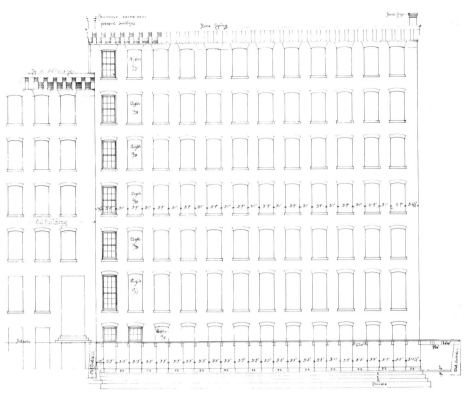

Mayer-Warenhaus   1892/93

Südwestecke Van Buren und Franklin Streets, Chicago;
1969 abgerissen

Hugh Morrison identifizierte das Gebäude als ein Werk
von Adler & Sullivan (1935, S. 168). Er fand seine Straßenfassaden bar jeder Ornamentierung vor und die tragende Eisenkonstruktion nur mit Backsteinen ummantelt.
Dies veranlaßte ihn, in diesem Bauwerk einen Vorläufer
des «International Style» zu sehen. Die publizierte per-
spektivische Zeichnung des Projekts zeigt allerdings, daß
ursprünglich ein anderer Ausdruck beabsichtigt war: Was
auf den ersten Blick wie eine kolossale Pfeilerordnung
wirkt, sind große, dekorierte Rahmen, die die übereinanderliegenden Fenster pro Joch zusammenfassen sollten;
was wie ein Fries unterhalb des Dachgesimses aussieht,
war als ein horizontal gerahmtes Fensterband gedacht.
Inwiewiet diese Dekorationen tatsächlich ausgeführt wurden, ist ungewiß, da das Gebäude vor der Identifizierung
durch Morrison möglicherweise umgebaut worden ist.

Mayer Warehouse   1892/93

Southwest corner of Van Buren and Franklin Streets,
Chicago; demolished in 1969

Hugh Morrison was the first to identify this building as a
work of Adler & Sullivan (1935, p. 168). The street front
utterly lacking ornament as well as the load-bearing iron-
frame construction sheathed only by an exterior wall of
brick led him to claim this building to be an early example
of the "International Style". However, the perspective
drawing of the project demonstrates that another style
was originally intended: what first appears to be a gigantic system of piers in the drawing is in effect a series of
large decorated frames that form long vertical bays of
double windows; what appears to be a frieze below the
cornice was nothing more than a frame of horizontal band
of windows. It is uncertain exactly how much of this ornament was actually executed, since the building may have
been remodelled before being discovered by Morrison.

Entwurf.
Project.

Zustand um 1935.
Condition around 1935.

Grabmal für Charlotte Wainwright 1892

Bellefontaine Cemetery, St. Louis, Missouri

Das Grabmonument – der «Taj Mahal» von St. Louis – wurde von Ellis Wainwright für seine jung verstorbene Frau in Auftrag gegeben. Wie üblich arbeitete Sullivan mit einfachen Bauvolumen. Auffällig ist vor allem das Ornamentband, das teils den Einschnitten der Öffnungen, teils den Rändern der Fassadenfläche folgt und solchermaßen Öffnungen und Flächen im Sinne einer «mariage des formes» verbindet. Sullivans Gestaltung unterscheidet sich wesentlich von den umstehenden Imitationen im ägyptischen, klassischen oder gotischen Stil, ist aber auch nicht ex nihilo entstanden – sowohl im volumetrischen Aufbau als auch im dekorativen Band offenbaren sich formale Anleihen bei byzantinischen Bauten.

Tomb for Charlotte Wainwright 1892

Bellefontaine Cemetery, St. Louis, Missouri

Ellis Wainwright commissioned this tomb – "the Taj Mahal of St. Louis" – for his wife, Charlotte, who died young. As usual, Sullivan worked with simple volumetric forms. Particularly distinctive is the ornamental carving that forms a decorative band around the openings as well as the top and sides of the façade, joining the openings and surfaces in a "marriage of forms". Sullivan's design is significantly different from the surrounding imitations of Egyptian, classical, or gothic style. Nevertheless, it was not built ex nihilo either: the volumetric structure as well as the decorative band reveal the formal influence of Byzantine buildings.

Photo von Richard Nickel.
Photo by Richard Nickel.

St.-Nicholas-Hotel   1892/93

Nordwestecke Locust und 8th Streets, St. Louis,
Missouri; 1973 abgerissen

Das St.-Nicholas-Hotel war das einzige erster Klasse in St.
Louis. Es besaß 120 Gästezimmer sowie zusätzliche kommerzielle Nutzungen im Erdgeschoß. Im siebten Geschoß,
unter dem steilen Giebeldach, befand sich ein großer Bankettsaal. Bloß einzelne Teile des Baukörpers (Erker und
Balkon) wurden mit geometrisch dekorierten Tonplatten
ausgezeichnet. 1903 brannte der Dachstuhl, danach wurden über dem siebten Geschoß vier weitere Stockwerke
hinzugefügt und mit einem Flachdach bedeckt.

St. Nicholas Hotel   1892/93

Northwest corner of Locust and 8th Streets, St. Louis,
Missouri; demolished in 1973

The St. Nicholas Hotel was the only first-class hotel in
St. Louis. It had 120 rooms as well as additional commercial space for business use on the first floor. There was a
large banquet hall on the seventh floor under the steep
gabled roof. Only parts of the volume (bay windows and
the balconies) were distinguished by terra-cotta tiles
richly carved with intricate geometric designs. In 1903 the
roof truss on the top floor was destroyed by fire. At that
time four more floors were added above the former
seventh floor and covered with a flat box-roof.

Zeichnung der Straßenfassaden.
Drawing of the street elevations.

Victoria-Hotel   1892/93

Chicago Heights, Illinois; 1961 abgerissen

Das Hotel entstand im Zusammenhang mit der Weltausstellung in Chicago von 1893. Es umfaßte 115 Gästezimmer sowie weitere kommerzielle Nutzungen im Erdgeschoß. Während die Fassade der unteren beiden Geschosse aus rötlichem Backstein bestand, wurde das oberste Geschoß mit gelbem Mörtel verputzt und mit je einem Streifen floraler und geometrischer Ornamente verziert.

Victoria Hotel   1892/93

Chicago Heights, Illinois; demolished in 1961

This hotel was built as part of the World Exposition in Chicago in 1893. It contained 115 rooms as well as additional commercial space for business use on the first floor. The two lower floors were of unadorned red brick. The upper floor was completely faced with geometrically carved stucco painted yellow with a narrow band of floral ornament at the base.

Photo von Henry Fuermann.
Photo by Henry Fuermann.

Union Trust Building   1892/93

Nordwestecke Oliver und 7th Streets, St. Louis, Missouri

Das Geschäftshaus entstand nur einen Block entfernt vom Wainwright Building. Im Gegensatz zu dessen strenger Komposition fallen hier ausgefallene Dekorationen – angeblich Sullivans «Gewohnheitssünde» (Jordy 1986, S. 96) – auf. Der Eingang erinnert an den «Golden Doorway» des Transportation Building, die Rahmen um die Rundfenster im ersten Obergeschoß sind üppig dekoriert und werden an den Gebäudeecken von geschoßhohen Greifen bewacht, die auf ihrer Brust Wappenschilder mit dekorativen Phantasien tragen. Das Motiv der Tierfiguren erscheint nochmals unterhalb des Dachgesimses in Form von wasserspeienden Raubkatzen und Löwenköpfen auf Brüstungsmedaillons. 1903 wurde das Gebäude gegen Norden um drei Achsen erweitert, 1924 wurden die Rundfenster straßenseitig entfernt.

Union Trust Building   1892/93

Northwest corner of Olivier and 7th Streets, St. Louis, Missouri

This office building was erected just a block away from the Wainwright Building. The distinctive decoration on this structure – supposedly Sullivan's "besetting sin" (Jordy, 1986, p. 96) – presents a rather striking contrast to its severe design. The entrance recalls the "Golden Doorway" of the Transportation Building. The round windows on the second floor surrounded with ornately decorated frames are guarded by griffins – one-story-high creatures standing vigilantly at the corners of the building, bearing decorative shields to their chests. This animal motif is found again below the cornice on medallions which contain large water-spewing bearcats and lion heads. In 1903 three bays were added on the north side of the building. In 1924 the round windows on the street front were completely removed.

Der Sockel, Photo von Henry Fuermann.
The socket, photo by Henry Fuermann.

Rechte Seite / *right page*:
Gesamtansicht von Südosten.
General view from southeast.

Chicago Stock Exchange Building   1893/94

Ecke La Salle und Washington Streets, Chicago;
1972 abgerissen

Der Bau des Stock Exchange Building wurde vom Financier Ferdinand W. Peck vorangetrieben. Ähnlich wie beim Schiller Building verlangten die an das Grundstück angrenzenden Bauten spezielle Vorsichtsmaßnahmen bei der Fundamentierung. Auf Rat des Brückenbauers General William S. Smith entschloß sich Adler, entlang der Westseite, angrenzend an das Gebäude des «Chicago Herald», erstmals im Hochbau die Technik der «caisson foundations» anzuwenden. Dadurch wurde die Gebäudelast punktförmig bis auf die Felsschicht in 30 Metern Tiefe abgeleitet und jede ungleichmäßige Setzung infolge ungleicher Belastung vermieden.

Zwei für die «Chicago School of Architecture» typische Formmerkmale wurden im oberen Teil der Fassaden miteinander kombiniert: erstens das seit den späten achtziger Jahren in Chicago häufig verwendete Erkerfenster, das die Vertikale akzentuiert; zweitens das sogenannte «Chicago window», ein dreiteiliges Fenster mit unbeweglichem mittlerem Flügel, das die Fassaden horizontal gliedert. Bezeichnend ist außerdem, daß Sullivan die Öffnungen des 2. und 3. Geschosses, hinter welchen sich unter anderem der Börsensaal befand, mit reichen Ornamenten rahmte. Auch die Erker und «Chicago windows» in den oberen Geschossen wurden von einem feinen Rahmenprofil umgeben.

1972 verlor Richard Nickel, der sich um die Erhaltung und Erforschung der Bauten von Adler & Sullivan sehr verdient gemacht hatte, im Bauschutt der Börse sein Leben, als er dort nach wertvollen Überresten suchte. Börsensaal und Portikus wurden 1981 unter der Aufsicht von John Vinci auf dem Gelände des Art Institute of Chicago rekonstruiert.

Chicago Stock Exchange Building   1893/94

Corner of La Salle and Washington Streets, Chicago;
demolished in 1972

The construction of the Chicago Stock Exchange Building was promoted by the Chicago financier Ferdinand W. Peck. As with the Schiller Building, the adjacent buildings requested that precautionary measures be taken when constructing the foundation. Following the advice of the bridge-builder, General William W. Smith, Adler employed "caisson foundations" for the very first time in building construction along the west wall of the building adjacent to the "Chicago Herald". By diverting the building load at various intervals down to bed-rock, 75 feet below the surface, inequalities in settlement due to unequal loading were prevented.

Two formal features, typical of mainstream "Chicago School of Architecture", were combined in the upper part of the façade: first, the bay window, used frequently in Chicago since the late 1880s to accent verticality; secondly, the so-called "Chicago window", a tripartite window with a fixed middle pane dividing the façade horizontally. Characteristically, Sullivan distinguished the second and third floors which housed the stock exchange room – the heart of the complex – by framing the openings with ornate decoration. The bay windows and "Chicago windows" were also accentuated by a slender moulding.

Richard Nickel, who played an important role in the preservation of and research on Adler & Sullivan buildings, died in 1972 while looking for valuable remains among the rubble of the stock exchange. Under the supervision of John Vinci, the stock exchange room and the portico were reconstructed (1981) in the grounds of the Art Institute of Chicago.

Wandabwicklung des Börsensaals, Zeichnungen von Vinci-Kenny Architects.
Elevations of the trading room, drawings by Vinci-Kenny Architects.

Illustration aus Harper's Weekly, 12. Januar 1895.
Illustration in Harper's Weekly, January 12th 1895.

Der rekonstruierte Börsensaal, Photo von Bob Thall.
The reconstructed trading room, photo by Bob Thall.

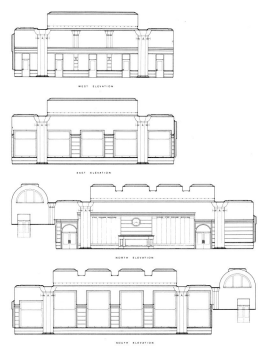

WEST ELEVATION

EAST ELEVATION

NORTH ELEVATION

SOUTH ELEVATION

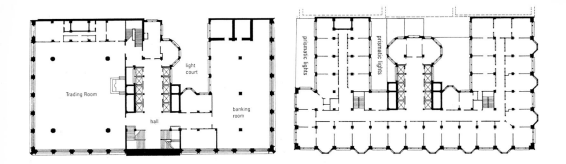

Grundriß des Obergeschosses mit Börsensaal und Normgrundriß zwischen 4. und 12. Geschoß.
Second floor plan with stock exchange trading room and typical plan for 4th–12th floors.

Fassade an der La Salle Street, Photos von Henry Fuermann.
Elevation on La Salle Street, photos by Henry Fuermann.

Guaranty (Prudential) Building   1894–1896

Südwestecke Pearl und Church Streets, Buffalo, New York

Kritiker sehen in diesem Bau einen «Zwilling» des Wainwright Building, wobei die Eleganz der Eisenkonstruktion in diesem Fall weit besser hinter den rötlichen Tonplatten zu erahnen sei. Claude Bragdon, der einzige wirkliche Schüler Sullivans, rühmte es als «the highest logical and aesthetic development of steel-framed building» (1909, S. 92). Ein Unternehmer namens Hascal T. Taylor wollte sich mit dem Gebäude ein Denkmal setzen. Als er 1894 plötzlich starb, übernahm die Guaranty-Baufirma das Projekt. Das Gebäude wurde am 1. März 1896 eröffnet. Fast gleichzeitig erschien Sullivans Essay «The Tall Office Building Artistically Articulated», worin er sein berühmtes Diktum «form follows function» begründete. Es ist nicht einfach, den Sinn dieses Satzes mit dem «all-over» der in Tonreliefs eingelassenen Ornamente an den Fassaden in Übereinstimmung zu bringen. Er erhält seine Bedeutung in diesem Zusammenhang erst, wenn man vom autonomen Status von Konstruktion und Dekoration ausgeht. Vollends scheinen hier die üppigen Dekorationen auf den akustischen Schalen der Auditorien von innen nach außen gestülpt zu sein. Sie machen weniger das konstruktive System sichtbar, als daß sie vielmehr den Stempel von Sullivans Imagination der Fassade aufdrücken (Wright 1924, S. 30). Sie überziehen die gesamte Fassade wie Hieroglyphen auf Säulen und Wänden des alten Ägypten. Doch Sullivans «Inschriften» beziehen sich auf die Gestalt der perforierten Hülle, genauer: auf die Übergänge zwischen innen und außen, die wie Bilder gerahmt werden. In diesem Sinne charakterisieren die Ornamente die individuelle Physiognomie des Bauwerks.

Die Konstruktion wird nur im Erdgeschoß sichtbar, wo die einfach ummantelten Säulen die Glaskästen der Schaufenster durchstoßen. Um die Helligkeit im Innern zu steigern, wurden das Treppenhaus und der Lichtschlitz gegen den Innenhof mit weißen, glasierten Backsteinen ausgekleidet, die um ein Mehrfaches teurer waren als normale Backsteine. Die Ausführung erfolgte bereits unter alleiniger Regie Sullivans, nachdem sich Adler Mitte 1895 zurückgezogen hatte. Angeblich hat Sullivan nachträglich Adlers Namen von allen Zeichnungen entfernt, was Adler zutiefst verletzte und schließlich Frank Lloyd Wrights Versuch, die beiden ehemaligen Partner wieder zusammenzubringen, scheitern ließ – «a heartbreaking situation» (Wright 1949, S. 87).

Guaranty (Prudential) Building   1894–1896

Southwest corner of Pearl and Church Streets, Buffalo, New York

Although this building is considered by critics to be the "twin" of the Wainwright Building, the elegance of the underlying steel-frame construction behind the red terracotta tiles is more apparent here than in the Wainwright. Claude Bragdon, Sullivan's only real student, claims it to be the "the highest logical and aesthetic development of steel-framed building". (1909, p. 92) The entrepreneur Hascal T. Taylor intended this building to be a monument to himself. After his sudden death in 1894, the Guaranty construction company took over the project. The building opened March 1, 1896. In his essay "The Tall Office Building Artistically Articulated", published at the same time, Sullivan explains his famous dictum: "form follows function". The meaning of this statement is not immediately evident in the context of the ornamental terra-cotta reliefs "all over" the façades. However, it can be understood, if one assumes that structure and ornament are autonomous. The lavish ornament on the acoustic ceiling panels in the auditoria seems almost as if turned inside out; the ornament is non-structural – it embellishes the surface, but it does not reveal the underlying structural system. Ornament is simply an imprint of Sullivan's imagination on the façade. (Wright 1924, p. 30) The entire façade of this building is clothed in ornament, like hieroglyphs on the columns and walls of temples in ancient Egypt. Sullivan's "inscriptions" actually outline the perforations of the exterior wall, the transitions between interior and exterior, by surrounding them with rich ornament like a picture frame. Thus, the purpose of the ornament lies in accentuating the individual physiognomy of the building.

Ornament is not intended to reveal the structure except on the first floor where the columns, sheathed with simple decoration, penetrate the projecting glass plate of the display windows. In order to increase the amount of light to the interior, the stairwell and the light slit facing the inner courtyard were lined with white glazed terra-cotta that was more costly than normal tiles. After Adler's retirement in 1895, Sullivan was left in charge of the project. Apparently, Sullivan had Adler's name subsequently removed from all the drawings. Adler was deeply hurt by this. Thus, Frank Lloyd Wright's attempt to re-form the partnership failed – "a heart-breaking situation" (Wright 1949, p. 87).

Photo von Henry Fuermann.
Photo by Henry Fuermann.

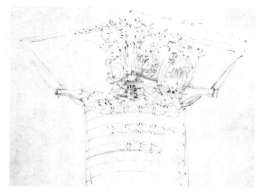

Zeichnung von Sullivan, 21. August 1895, Bleistift auf Briefpapier, 27,5 × 20 cm.
Drawing by Sullivan, August 21st 1895, pencil on stationery, 27,5 × 20 cm.

Säulenkapitell aus Terrakotta.
Terra-cotta capital.

Normgrundriß.
Typical floor plan.

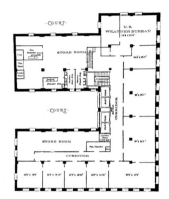

Ladenfront und Treppenhaus, Photos von Henry Fuermann.
Storefront and staircase, photos by Henry Fuermann.

Lobby, Photo von Patricia Layman Bazelon.
Lobby, photo by Patricia Layman Bazelon.

Bayard (später Condict) Building   1897–1899
65 Bleecker Street, New York
Sullivan hielt dieses Werk für das beste unter allen seinen Geschäftshochhäusern. Neben den früheren Beispielen macht es den Eindruck einer «übertrieben herausgeputzten Lady» (Jordy 1986, S. 113). Neu sind die Übergänge von Sockel, Schaft und Dachgesimse, ebenso die an gotische Doppelfenster erinnernde vertikale Zusammenfassung der Bürofenster. Die gotischen Formen sind aber insofern modifiziert, als das Stabwerk nicht bis zur Basis hinunterführt und die Profile der Gewände wie Rahmenwerke die Öffnungen umfassen. Auch hier sind die dekorierten und profilierten Tonplatten nicht unmittelbarer Ausdruck der Konstruktion, sondern vielmehr eine Art Maske, die die konstruktiven und funktionellen Gegebenheiten in eine individuelle und charakteristische äußere Form überträgt.

Bayard (later Condict) Building   1897–1899
65 Bleecker Street, New York
Sullivan considered this the best of all his tall office buildings. Compared to his earlier works, this building looks like an "over-dressed lady" (Jordy, 1986, p. 113). The transitions between base, shaft and roof cornice, as well as the vertically combined office windows (reminiscent of gothic double windows) are new features. The gothic forms have been somewhat modified, in that the mullions do not extend to the base and the moldings of the window jambs surround the large vertical openings like framework. Also, here the ornamental and embossed tiles are not a direct expression of the underlying structure; they act more as a kind of mask giving the structural and functional features of the building an individual and characteristic external form.

Details der Fassade, Schnitt und Gesamtansicht.
Details of the elevation, section and general view.

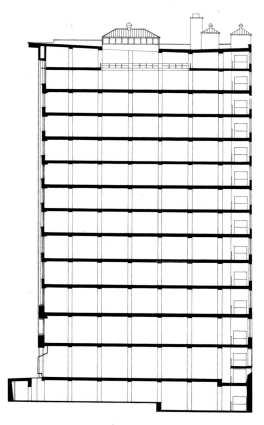

Gage Building   1898/99

18 South Michigan Avenue, Chicago

Den Bauauftrag für das Modezentrum, das Stanley McCormick an einer der attraktivsten Hauptstraßen Chicagos errichten wollte, erhielten Holabird & Roche. Entsprechend der Zahl und Größe der vorgesehenen Geschäfte teilten sie den Komplex in drei voneinander unabhängige, gegen Süden abgetreppte Einheiten. Gage Brothers & Co. verlangten vom Bauherrn ein ihrer Firma entsprechendes Äußeres, wofür sie einen Aufpreis zu zahlen bereit waren. Zu diesem Zwecke wurde nun Sullivan zugezogen: Im Gegensatz zu Holabird & Roche, die die riesigen Öffnungen des Skelettbaus mit «Chicago-Fenstern» ausfachten, teilte er diese horizontal in je einen Streifen mit Brüstung, Fensterglas und «Luxfer»-Glasbausteinen. Diesen horizontalen Bändern blendete er als vertikale Akzente zwei Stengel aus Terrakotta vor, die beide unter dem Dachgesimse in einem üppigen Ausbund von Ornamenten enden. Die besonders reichen Ornamente im Ladengeschoß wurden von Sullivan entworfen, von Kristian Schneider in Ton modelliert und bei Winslow Brothers in gußeiserne Formen gegossen. 1902 wurde Sullivans Teil des Gebäudekomplexes um vier Geschosse aufgestockt, allerdings nicht mehr durch Sullivan, sondern durch Holabird & Roche. Diese hielten sich genau an Sullivans Vorgaben und ließen die Ornamentsträuße unter dem Dachgesimse entsprechend in die Höhe liften.

Gage Building   1898/99

18 South Michigan Avenue, Chicago

Stanley McCormick commissioned Holabird & Roche to design a fashion center on one of the most stylish streets in downtown Chicago. According to the planned number and size of the firms, the complex was divided into three independent units, staggered in height, extending from north to south. Gage Brothers & Co. were willing to pay an additional charge for an exterior design that would be more appropriate to their millinery business. Sullivan was selected to design the façade: unlike Holabird & Roche who simply filled the gigantic openings of the building's skeletal structure with "Chicago windows", he divided the openings into horizontal bands of parapets and windows coupled with a band of "Luxfer" glass blocks. As vertical accents, he superimposed two terra-cotta mullions onto the horizontal bands that end in a burst of ornamental foliage just below the cornice. The especially rich ornament of the mercantile shops at the street level was also designed by Sullivan. Kristian Schneider made the terra-cotta molds which were then cast in iron by the Winslow Brothers. In 1902 four more floors were added to the building Sullivan designed. Although Holabird & Roche drew the plans for this addition, they followed Sullivan's design in detail, even raising the bouquets of ornamental foliage under the cornice and repositioning them on the top floor of the building.

Während der Bauarbeiten.
Under construction.

Ladenfront an der Michigan Avenue.
Storefront on Michigan Avenue.

McCormicks Modezentrum von Holabird & Roche, rechts die von Sullivan gestaltete Fassade vor der Aufstockung 1902.
McCormick's fashion centre by Holabird & Roche, on the right Sullivan's design prior to addition 1902.

Holy Trinity Cathedral   1899–1903

1121 North Leavitt, Chicago

Im Gegensatz zu den Entwürfen für mondäne Warenhäuser im Zentrum von Chicago bedeutete dieser Auftrag eine Begegnung mit einer alten religiösen Tradition. Die Komposition der Baumassen, die farbige Gestaltung im Innern, die geschnitzten Fensterrahmen und Gesimse sowie der Turmhelm lassen einen an ländliche Kirchen in Rußland denken, ohne daß Sullivan ein bestimmtes Vorbild nachgeahmt hätte. Manche Autoren sind der Meinung, daß Sullivan in diesem Zusammenhang «L'art russe» (1877) von Viollet-le-Duc studiert habe. (In Sullivans Bibliothek befand sich wohl ein Werk dieses großen zeitgenössischen Theoretikers und Architekten, allerdings nicht jenes über russische Kunst.) Sullivan verzichtete auf die Hälfte seines Honorars in der Hoffnung, das Äußere der Kirche im Stile des Transportation Building farbig gestalten zu können, jedoch ohne Erfolg.

Holy Trinity Cathedral   1899–1903

1121 North Leavitt, Chicago

This commission for a religious building was quite a departure from the chic department stores in downtown Chicago. Although not consciously emulating a particular style, the design of the building, the colorful handling of the interior, the carved window frames and cornices as well as the spire are reminiscent of a provincial church in Russia. Some authors claim that Sullivan studied Violett-le-Duc's "L'art russe" while working on this project. (A book by this great contemporary architect and theoretician was found in Sullivan's library, but it was not the one about Russian art.) Hoping to design a colorful exterior for the church similar to that of the Transportation Building, Sullivan waived half of his fee, but unfortunately he was not able to carry this out.

Ansicht der Kirche mit Pfarrhaus.
General view of the cathedral and parish house.

Grundriß und Ansicht des Innern.
Floor plan and interior.

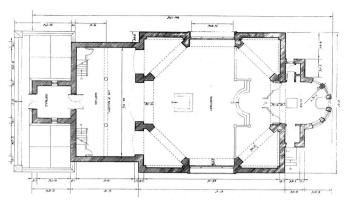

Schlesinger-&-Mayer- (heute Carson-Pirie-Scott-) Warenhaus   1885, 1896, 1899, 1902/03

Südostecke State und Madison Streets, Chicago

1881 verlegten Leopold Schlesinger und David Mayer ihr Warenhaus in ein bestehendes Gebäude an «The World Busiest Corner», von wo aus das gesamte Straßensystem Chicagos numeriert ist. Adler & Sullivan wurden ab 1885 mit verschiedenen inneren Erweiterungen und Renovationen beauftragt. 1896 sollte dann auf der Westseite des Blocks ein Anschluß an die neue Loop-Hochbahn geschaffen werden. Der Auftrag ging an Sullivan – dies ist der einzige Fall, wo ehemalige Kunden von Adler & Sullivan sich nach Auflösung der Firma an Sullivan wandten. Die Pläne wurden von George Elmslie gezeichnet, der 1893 die Nachfolge von Wright antrat und bis 1909 bei Sullivan blieb. Vom schmalen, zehngeschossigen Bau an der Wabash Avenue wurden nur die ersten beiden Geschosse und die Passerelle zur Haltestelle realisiert. Der Umbau des Warenhauses der Mandel Brothers von 1898 auf der gegenüberliegenden Seite der Madison Street bewog Schlesinger & Mayer ihrerseits zur Ankündigung eines Neubaus. Sullivan mußte sein zunächst zwölfgeschossiges Projekt aus baurechtlichen Gründen auf neun Geschosse reduzieren. 1899 begann man mit dem Bau der ersten drei Joche entlang der Madison Street. Die geplanten edlen Bronzerahmen der Schaufenster mußten allerdings durch billigere gußeiserne Rahmen ersetzt werden, wie auch die oberen Geschosse nicht mit weißen Marmorplatten, sondern bloß mit weiß glasierten Tontafeln verkleidet werden konnten.

Nachdem 1902 in Chicago die zulässige Bauhöhe auf beinahe 75 Meter verdoppelt wurde, reichte Sullivan ein neues Projekt mit zwölf Geschossen ein, dessen Aufbau mit dem des bereits bestehenden Trakts identisch war. Über dem neunten Stockwerk wurde die Geschoßhöhe reduziert, das Dachgeschoß besaß straßenseitig eine durchgehende Loggia, über der die stirnseitig verzierte Dachplatte weit auskragte. Die Dreiteilung der Fassade insgesamt entspricht der klassischen Tektonik (Sockel, Schaft, Kapitell), wurde jedoch von Sullivan umgedeutet, indem er die Teile als dekorierte Rahmen voneinander unterschied und den unteren Rahmen jeweils vor den oberen vorspringen ließ. Der Zylinder an der Straßenecke zeichnet sich durch vertikale Streben aus und verbindet wie ein Scharnier die beiden Flügel entlang der Madison und State Streets mit ihren horizontalen «Chicago-Fenstern».

Schlesinger & Mayer (today Carson Pirie Scott) Department Store   1885, 1896, 1899, 1902/03

Southeast corner of State and Madison Streets, Chicago

In 1881 Leopold Schlesinger and David Mayer moved their department store into an existing building on the "The World's Busiest Corner", the point from which all the streets in Chicago are numbered. From 1885 on, Adler & Sullivan were engaged to design various interior additions and to renovate the existing building. In 1896 an extension was to be built on the west side of the block next to Chicago's Loop. Sullivan was selected as the architect – this was the only time former clients of Adler-& Sullivan consulted Sullivan after the partnership had dissolved. The plans were drawn up by George Elmslie who had taken over Wright's position in the firm as chief designer. He remained with Sullivan until 1909. Of the narrow ten-story building initially planned on Wabash Avenue, only the first two floors and the passerelle to the bus stop were actually built. The remodelling of the Mandel Brothers Department Store in 1898 on the opposite side of Madison Street inspired Schlesinger & Mayer to draw up plans for an entirely new building. First, Sullivan's initial plan for a twelve-story building had to be reduced to nine floors due to building restrictions. Construction began with the first of three bays on Madison Street in 1899. The frames around the display windows, originally planned in an exquisite bronze, had to be replaced with less expensive cast iron. In addition, the upper stories were sheathed in a casing of white-glazed terra-cotta tablets instead of white marble plates.

When the building limit in Chicago was nearly doubled to 240 feet in 1902, Sullivan submitted a new project with twelve stories, identical in design to the existing block, although the height of each story above the ninth floor was reduced. The top story facing the street constisted of a continuous loggia topped by a large overhanging roof slab faced with ornament. Although the tripartite division of the façade essentially corresponds to classical tectonics (base, shaft, capital), Sullivan reinterpreted the parts of this system by distinguishing them as decorated frames which were recessed successively from the base to the capital. Due to its distinctive verticality, the cylindrical pavilion on the street corner acts as a great hinge, joining the two wings along Madison and State Streets with their horizontal "Chicago windows".

The second phase of construction began in October 1902.

Mit dieser zweiten Etappe wurde im Oktober 1902 begonnen. Zunächst wurden 59 «caisson foundations» vom Keller aus in den Boden getrieben, während in den Ladengeschossen der Weihnachtsrummel losging. Sullivan publizierte dieses technische Bravourstück postwendend in «The Engineering Record» vom Februar 1903. Nach Weihnachten wurde das bestehende Gebäude abgerissen, das Eisenskelett in Rekordzeit aufgestellt und bis Mai 1903 bezugsbereit ausgebaut. Die dritte Etappe umfaßte eine Verlängerung der Front entlang der State Street gegen Süden um weitere vier Joche. Noch während diese Etappe im Bau war, ging das Warenhaus in den Besitz von Carson Pirie Scott über, deren Geschäft bislang im Reliance Building (Burnham & Root, Atwood) untergebracht war. Als sie ihrerseits das neu erworbene Gebäude nach Süden erweitern wollten, gelang es Daniel Burnham, den Auftrag an sich zu reißen. Er mußte sich jedoch an die Vorgaben von Sullivans Gestaltung halten, außer daß er auf die dekorierten Rahmen der «Chicago-Fenster» verzichtete und die Loggia im Dachgeschoß nicht weiterführte. 1948 wurde an Sullivans Teil die Loggia inklusive Dachabschluß verändert.

First, 59 "caisson foundations" were driven from the basement into the ground in the midst of the hustle and bustle of Christmas shopping in the department stores. Sullivan immediately published this technical feat in "The Engineering Record" of February, 1903. After Christmas, the existing building was torn down. The steel skeleton-frame was erected in record time, and by May 1903 the building was ready to be occupied. The third phase of construction consisted of extending the front four more bays southward on State Street. Before the building was completed, the department store was sold to Carson Pirie Scott whose business had previously been housed in the Reliance Building (Burnham & Root, Atwood). After acquiring the new building, they wanted to add yet another extension to the south. Although Daniel Burnham succeeded in getting the contract, he had to follow Sullivan's original design. Except for the ornamental window frames and the loggia on the top story, the design is in every detail the same as the previous structure. The loggia as well as the roof projection on Sullivan's building were remodelled in 1948.

Lageplan, Grundstückerwerb von Schlesinger & Mayer.
Site plan, property acquisitions of Schlesinger & Mayer.

Während der Bauarbeiten, 23. März 1903.
Under construction, March 23, 1903.

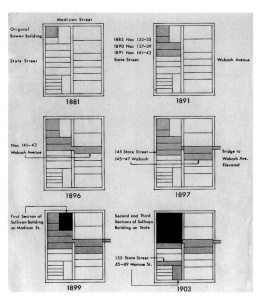

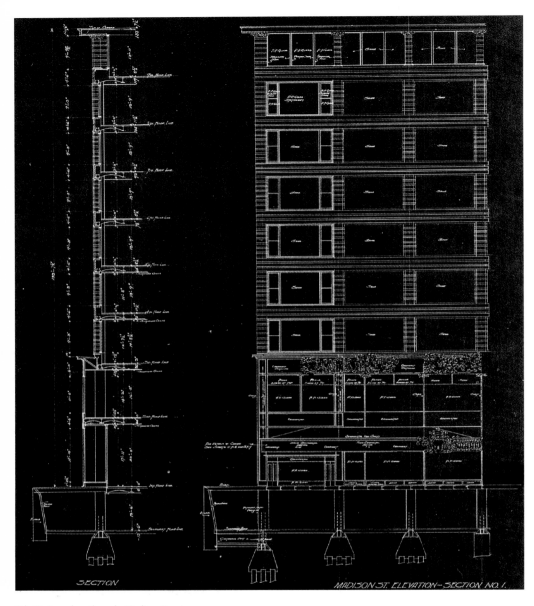

Schnitt, Fassade entlang der Madison Street.
Section, Madison Street elevation.

Ecke State/Madison Street.
Corner State/Madison Street.

Ladenfront,
Photos von Henry Fuermann.
Storefront,
photos by Henry Fuermann.

Abbildung in Sigfried Giedions
«Raum, Zeit, Architektur»
(«auffallend ob seiner
kraftvollen und klaren
Gestaltung . . .»).
*Illustration in Sigfried
Giedion's «Space, Time and
Architecture» («outstanding
for strength and purity of
expression . . .»).*

Abbildung in Juan Bontas
«Über Interpretation von
Architektur».
*Illustration in Juan Bonta's
«Architecture and its
interpretation».*

National Farmers' Bank   1906–1908

Nordostecke Broadway und Cedar Street, Owatonna, Minnesota

Der kulturell interessierte Bankier Carl K. Bennett las Sullivans Artikel «What is Architecture? A Study in the American People of Today» (1906). Er vermochte das Direktorium seiner Bank zu überzeugen, Sullivan mit dem geplanten Neubau zu beauftragen. Sullivans rigorose Ablehnung klassischer Bauformen als «leere Chitinhüllen» ließ sich an Ort und Stelle auf das gegenüberliegende Gebäude der Konkurrenz beziehen und einen neuen, eigenständigen Ausdruck der modernen amerikanischen Zivilisation erwarten. Zwar ist auch Sullivans Bau analog dem Prinzip der klassischen Dreiteilung gegliedert, doch die Gestalt jedes Teils wurde neu interpretiert: die Sockelprofile werden zu Fensterlaibungen, die großen Lünettenfenster werden wie Gemälde durch ornamentale Bänder und Lüster gerahmt, und das Dachgesims scheint den Bau gegen den Himmel eher zu öffnen als abzuschließen. Sullivan bevorzugte rauhe, farblich vielfältige Backsteine («tapestry» oder «oriental brick»), weil sie im Verband wie ein alter anatolischer Teppich wirken (vergleiche dazu Frampton im Vorwort zu Weingarden 1987). Das Hauptvolumen umschließt eine einzige zentrale Halle, die durch gemauerte Zwischenwände in funktionelle Zonen unterteilt wurde.

Der Gestaltung des Innern kommt große Bedeutung zu, da Sullivan hier, wie er im April 1908 an Bennett schrieb, eine «Farbsymphonie» beabsichtigte: Er versuchte, «to make out-of-doors indoors», wobei die verschiedenen Farbtöne der Fenster, der Wanddekorationen und der beiden Wandgemälde miteinander harmonieren sollten. Insgesamt wurden 60 verschiedene Arten von Ornamenten für Schablonenbemalung, Tür- und Fensterprofile, Leuchter, Schaltergitter etc. entworfen. Louis L. Millet, mit dem Sullivan schon beim Auditorium zusammengearbeitet hatte, übernahm die Bemalung der Wände mit Schablonenmustern. Von Oskar Gross, einem gebürtigen Wiener, stammen die beiden Wandbilder, die auf Owatonnas damalige wirtschaftliche Basis («the butter capital of the world») anspielen. Schon bald wurde die Bank zum «Mekka für Architektur-Pilger», wie der Architekturkritiker des «Architectural Record», Montgomery Schuyler, 1909 schrieb. Einer der führenden Architekten Europas, der Holländer Hendrik P. Berlage reiste 1911 eigens nach Owatonna, um das Meisterwerk «mit einer Kraft, die jedem Kunstwerk würdig ist», mit eigenen Augen zu begut-

National Farmers' Bank   1906–1908

Northeast corner of Broadway and Cedar Street, Owatonna, Minnesota

The vice-president of the National Farmer's Bank, Carl K. Bennett, whose interest in architecture prompted him to read Sullivan's article "What is Architecture? A Study in the American People of Today" (1906), persuaded the board of directors to engage Sullivan to design the new building. Sullivan's adamant rejection of classical forms as an "empty carcass", an implied critique of their competitor's building on the opposite side of the street, aroused expectations of a new and unique expression of modern American civilization. Even though Sullivan's building followed the classical principle of tripartite structuring, the form of each part was interpreted in a new way: the moldings on the base become the projecting reveals of the windows; the great arched windows become pictures framed by courses of brick and ornamental bands; the cornice seems to extend the building upward rather than delimiting it. Sullivan preferred a rough shale brick facing with variegated colors, "tapestry" or "oriental brick", because at a distance it creates the effect of an Anatolian rug (cf. Frampton in the preface to Weingarden, 1987). The interior of the building encompasses one central lobby functionally subdivided into various working areas by brick enclosures.

As Sullivan explained in a letter to Bennett in April 1908, the interior of the building was of the utmost importance, for he intended to create a "symphony in color": he tried "to make out-of-doors indoors". Thus, he combined the various shades of color used in the windows, the wall decoration and both of the mural paintings to create an harmonious atmosphere. A total of 60 different types of ornament were designed for stencil painting, door and window moldings, chandeliers, cashiers' grilles and tellers' wickets, etc. Louis L. Millet, who had worked with Sullivan on the Auditorium, was responsible for painting the stencilled patterns on the walls. The two mural paintings whose themes allude to Owatonna's main industry and source of income at that time ("the butter capital of the world") were painted by Oskar Gross from Vienna. As Montgomery Schuyler, the architectural critic of the "Architectural Record", wrote in 1909, the bank very quickly became "Mecca for architectural pilgrims". One of the leading architects in Europe, the Dutchman Hendrik P. Berlage, traveled to Owatonna in 1911 specifically to examine the building with his own eyes: a masterpiece

achten (Berlage 1912, S. 150). 1981 wurde die Bank als eines von insgesamt 16 Bauwerken für die Briefmarkenserie «Architecture USA» ausgewählt. Alle erhaltenen Zeichnungen bis auf den Entwurf eines Schablonenmusters für die Wandbemalung sind von George Elmslie. Sein Anteil am Entwurf ist in diesem Fall offen und am meisten umstritten.

whose "strength was worthy of any work of art" (Berlage, 1912, p. 150). In 1981, the National Farmer's Bank was one of a total of 16 buildings selected for the stamp series "Architecture USA". All of the existing drawings except for one stencil pattern were executed by George Elmslie. How much he actually did contribute to the design is not clear and remains a subject of controversy.

Grundriß.
Floor plan.

Briefmarken der Serie «Architecture USA», 1981; 4 von 16 Bauten.
Stamps of the series «Architecture USA», 1981; 4 out of 16 buildings.

Photo von Henry Fuermann.
Photo by Henry Fuermann.

Photo von Eduard S. Cunningham.
Photo by Eduard S. Cunningham.

Detail von Fassadenornamenten, Photo von Henry Fuermann.
Detail of facade ornaments, photo by Henry Fuermann.

Sockelzone.
Socket.

132

Schalterhalle, Photos von
Henry Fuermann (oben) und
Warren Reynolds (unten).
*Banking lobby, photos by
Henry Fuermann (above) and
Warren Reynolds (below).*

Vergnügungspark Island City   1907

Petty's Island, Philadelphia, Pennsylvania; Projekt

Die Idee wurde von Geschäftsleuten aus New York und Philadelphia ersonnen. Auf der Insel im Delaware standen 1,4 km^2 Land zur Verfügung: Sullivan bestückte die Anlage mit einem Hafen, einem Schwimmbad, einem großen Hotel inklusive Banketräumen, mit Cafés sowie einem Theater und einem Schiffsmuseum. Die meisten Nutzungen waren entlang einer breiten zentralen Achse vorgesehen, die durch Arkaden, dekorierte Pylonen und Fahnen eine festliche Stimmung verbreiten sollten.

Island City Amusement Park   1907

Petty's Island, Philadelphia, Pennsylvania; project

This project was the brainchild of businessmen from New York and Philadelphia. They had an area of 344 acres on Petty's Island in Delaware to build the park. Sullivan equipped the complex with a port, a swimming pool, a large hotel which included banquet halls, cafés as well as a theater and a nautical museum. Most of the spaces were arranged along a wide central axis accented with arcades, ornamental pylons and flags to create a festive atmosphere.

Zeichnung aus der Vogelperspektive.
Prospective of areal view.

Fassadenzeichnungen.
Elevation drawings.

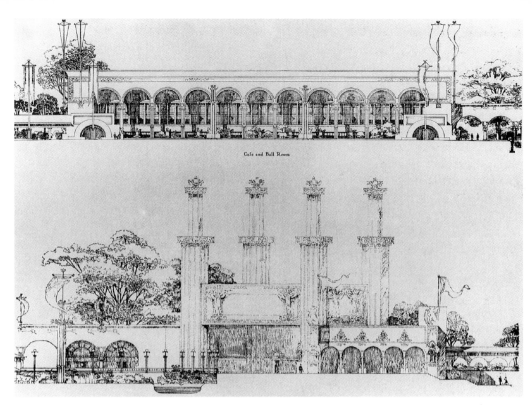

Cafe and Ball Room

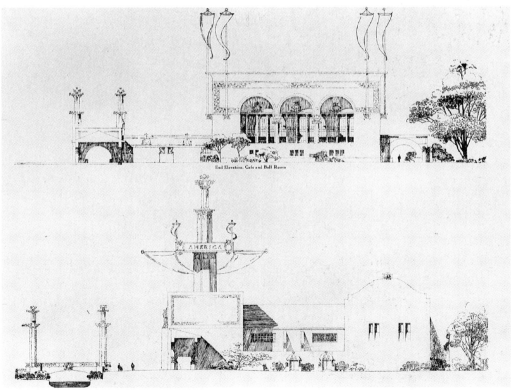

End Elevation, Cafe and Ball Room

Haus Babson   1907–1909

230 Riverside Drive 208, Riverside, Illinois;
1960 abgerissen

Von allen Wohnbauprojekten, an welchen Sullivan nach der Trennung von Adler arbeitete, war jenes für die Familie von James Babson das konventionellste, aber auch das bequemste. Vielleicht weil sich der Architekt hier am engsten an die räumliche Konzeption der frühen Bauten der «Prairie School» von Frank Lloyd Wright hielt, etwa das berühmte («battleship») Robie House von 1906 in Chicago. Die Ähnlichkeiten könnten sich unmittelbar aus der Tatsache ergeben haben, daß Sullivans Bürovorsteher George Elmslie öfters in Wrights Büro in Oak Park aushalf. 1911 erschien in «The Architectural Record» unter dem Titel «A Departure from Classic Tradition – Two Unusual Houses by Louis Sullivan and Frank Lloyd Wright, Architects» ein reich bebilderter Vergleich zwischen dem Babson-Haus und dem Coonley-Haus, das Wright zur gleichen Zeit nur wenige Straßen entfernt errichtete. Sullivans Entwurf ist weniger homogen, vor allem wenn man beachtet, wie sich der reich dekorierte Balkon auf der Westseite vom Baukörper aus Backstein abhebt.

Babson House   1907–1909

230 Riverside Drive 208, Riverside, Illinois;
demolished in 1960

Of all the residential projects that Sullivan designed after separating from Adler, the house for the James Babson family was the most conventional but also the most comfortable, probably because here the architect adhered most closely to the spatial concept of the early buildings of the "Prairie School" of Frank Lloyd Wright, such as his famous ("battleship") Robie House built in Chicago, 1906. These similarities could have been a direct result of the fact that George Elmslie, Sullivan's chief designer, often assisted in Wright's office in Oak Park. In 1911 a well-illustrated article comparing the Babson House and the Coonley House, which Wright was building at the same time only a few blocks away, was published in the "The Architectural Record" under the title "A Departure from the Classic Tradition – Two Unusual Houses by Louis Sullivan and Frank Lloyd Wright, Architects". Sullivan's design is not as homogeneous as Wright's, especially taking into account how the ornately decorated balcony on the west side contrasts with the brick structure.

Grundrisse.
Floor plans.

Rechte Seite / *right page*:
Gartenfassade und Halle,
Photos von Henry Fuermann.
Garden elevation and hall,
photos by Henry Fuermann.

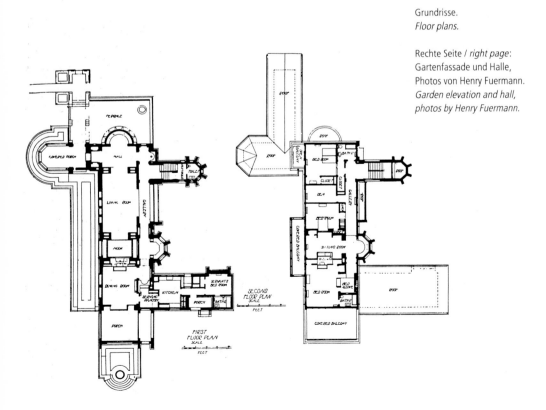

Haus Bradley   1908–1910

106 N. Prospect Street, Madison, Wisconsin

Charles Crane, der Besitzer einer Aufzugsfirma in Chicago, mit dem Adler & Sullivan seit dem Auditorium verschiedentlich zusammengearbeitet hatten, ließ Sullivan ein Wohnhaus für die Familie seiner Tochter Josephine projektieren. Der erste Vorschlag wurde Ende 1908 von der Familie als zu repräsentativ abgelehnt. Das zweite Projekt jedoch wurde ausgeführt, obwohl auch es der Familie immer noch zu groß erschien. Der Bauherr erinnerte sich später: «Sullivan, who was to begin with the polished courtly gentlemen, whom we enjoyed in spite of his insistence on dominating the plans, seemed deteriorate.» Nachdem George Elmslie im November 1909 Sullivans Büro verlassen mußte, übernahm er zusammen mit seinen neuen Partnern in Madison die Ausführung des Baus. Trotzdem bestätigte er, daß der Entwurf gänzlich Sullivan zugeschrieben werden müsse (Elmslie 1936 in einem offenen Brief an Frank Lloyd Wright). Wright hatte zu dieser Zeit in der gleichen Stadt, nur einige Straßen vom Bradley-Haus entfernt, mit dem Bau des Gilmore-Hauses («airplane house») begonnen, wo er mit einem vergleichbaren technischen Imponierstück aufwartete, wie Sullivan mit seinen mächtigen Konsolen, welche die Flügel des «Querschiffs» tragen. Die Bradleys ließen sich bereits 1914/15 von Purcell & Elmslie ein bescheideneres Haus bauen und verkauften das alte an die Sigma-Bruderschaft, die es heute noch besitzt.

Bradley House   1908–1910

106 N. Prospect Street, Madison, Wisconsin

Charles Crane was the owner of an elevator company in Chicago with whom Adler & Sullivan had worked on several occasions since the Auditorium. He had Sullivan draw up plans for a residence for the family of his daughter, Josephine. The first version, designed late in 1908, was rejected by the family as being too prestigious. The second version was finally executed, even though it still seemed too large for their needs. The client later remembered Sullivan thus: "Sullivan, who was to begin with the polished courtly gentlemen, whom we enjoyed in spite of his insistence on dominating the plans, seemed to deteriorate." After leaving Sullivan's firm in November 1909, George Elmslie took over the construction of the building with his new partners in Madison. Nevertheless, he did confirm that the design conception is "wholly Sullivan's" (Elmslie, in a open letter to F. L. Wright, 1936). At that time, a few blocks away from the Bradley House, Frank Lloyd Wright had just begun building the Gilmore House ("airplane house"), where he offered a technically impressive feat comparable to Sullivan's powerful corbels supporting the wings of the "transept". The Bradleys had Purcell & Elmslie build them a more modest home in 1914/15, and they sold the old one to the present owner, the Sigma Fraternity.

Grundriß des Erdgeschosses, erste Variante und gebaute Version.
First floor plans, first proposal and executed version.

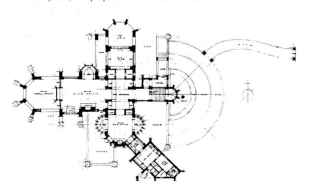
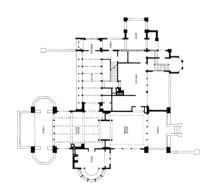

Peoples Savings Bank   1909–1911

Südwestecke 3rd Avenue und 1st Street, S. W.,
Cedar Rapids, Iowa

Vom Erfolg der Bank in Owatonna angezogen, wandte sich auch der Präsident der expandierenden Peoples Savings Bank in Cedar Rapids, H. E. Witwer, an Sullivan. Die zentrale Halle ist von Büros und Serviceräumen umgeben und erhält Tageslicht durch die Öffnungen im Lichtgaden. Darunter, in der Zone des Triphoriums, befinden sich vier Wandgemälde von Allen E. Philbrick, der am Art Institute of Chicago unterrichtete. Sie zeigen die Jahreszeiten in Verbindung mit den vier ökonomischen Grundlagen von Iowa: Industrie, Bankwesen, Handel, Landwirtschaft.

Dem übersteigerten Sicherheitsbedürfnis entspricht die Tresortür, mit über 2 Meter Durchmesser, 61 Zentimeter dick und rund 25 Tonnen schwer, die Sullivan gut sichtbar genau dem Eingang gegenüber plazierte. Im Innern waren die Safes mit Spiegelglas versehen, was den Raum in eine Art «Palast der Illusionen» verwandelte. «The building is thus clearly designed from within outward. The exterior is the envelope of the interior reduced to the very simplest expression», schrieb Montgomery Schuyler 1912 in einer Kritik. Den abgetreppten volumetrischen Aufbau verstärkte Sullivan dadurch, daß er den Rand des Gehsteiges mit vier Beleuchtungspfosten markierte, die mit den Belüftungspylonen an den Ecken des Lichtgadens korrespondieren.

Peoples Savings Bank   1909–1911

Southwest corner of 3rd Avenue and 1st Street, S. W.,
Cedar Rapids, Iowa

Attracted by the success of the bank in Owatonna, the president of the expanding Peoples Savings Bank in Cedar Rapids, H. E. Witwer, consulted Sullivan. The bank consists of a central lobby surrounded by offices and work rooms lighted by a row of windows in the clerestory. Below the clerestory in the area of the triforium are four mural paintings by Allen E. Philbrick, teacher at the Art Institute of Chicago. They depict the four seasons in conjunction with the four pillars of the economy of Iowa: industry, banking, commerce, and agriculture.

The vault door, plainly visible opposite the entrance, is indicative of the exaggerated need for security: it is over 7 feet in diameter, 2 feet thick, and weighs 25 tons. Inside the vault, the safes were covered with mirrors creating a kind of "Palace of Illusions". According to Montgomery Schuyler in a critique from 1912: "The building is thus clearly designed from within outward. The exterior is the envelope of the interior reduced to the very simplest expression". The bank was conceived in terms of volumes recessed in steps which Sullivan emphasized by placing four lamp-posts at the edge of the walkway that served to accent the ventilation pylons positioned at the corners of the clerestory.

Straßenfassaden.
Street elevations.

Schalterhalle.
Banking lobby.

Tresortüre.
Safety deposit vault.

Grundriß.
Floor plan.

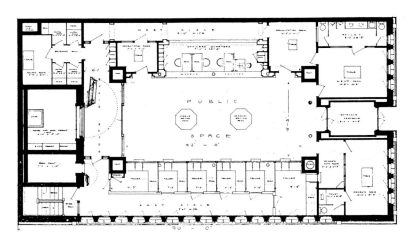

St. Paul's Methodist Episcopal Church
1910–1914

Ecke 3rd Avenue und 14th Street, S. E., Cedar Rapids, Iowa

Sullivan erhielt den Auftrag als Sieger eines Wettbewerbs, an dem unter anderen auch Purcell Feick & Elmslie teilgenommen hatten. Der holländische Architekt Hendrik P. Berlage, der die Pläne anläßlich eines Besuches bei Sullivan sah, schrieb darüber: «Sullivan hat jedoch den Mut gehabt, dem Kirchenraum die Form eines Halbkreises zu geben und den Turm in den Mittelpunkt desselben, also gewissermaßen über die Kanzel, zu stellen. Dieses letztere scheint mir um so bemerkenswerter, als dadurch der Turm eine höhere ethische Bedeutung erlangt.» Das Motiv der Engelsfiguren hatte Sullivan zuvor beim Transportation Building und beim Bayard Building verwendet; hier erinnern sie jedoch ausgesprochen an die symbolische Gestaltung Henry H. Richardsons für die Brattle Square Church in Boston. Als praktisch einzigen Bau, der ihm in seiner Studienzeit Eindruck gemacht hat, erwähnt Sullivan ihn in «The Autobiography of an Idea» (1924, S. 188). 1912 wurde das Projekt als zu kostspielig an Sullivan zur Bearbeitung zurückgesandt. Dieser weigerte sich jedoch, die verlangten Änderungen vorzunehmen. Der Auftrag wurde William C. Jones, einem Kirchenbauer aus Chicago, übergeben, dessen Pläne schließlich von Elmslie unentgeltlich nochmals im Sinne der ursprünglichen Konzeption überarbeitet wurden.

St. Paul's Methodist Episcopal Church
1910–1914

Corner of 3rd Avenue and 14th Street, S. E., Cedar Rapids, Iowa

Sullivan was engaged as architect for the new church building, after winning a competition which included, among others, Purcell, Feick & Elmslie. The Dutch architect Hendrik P. Berlage, who had seen the plans when visiting Sullivan, wrote: "Sullivan had the courage to design the church in the form of a semi-circle, placing the tower in the center of the space practically over the pulpit. The latter seems that much more remarkable, for it lends the tower a higher moral significance." Sullivan had previously employed the motif of the angels on the Transportation Building and the Bayard Building; however, here they recall of all things a symbolic treatment similar to the Brattle Square Church in Boston by Henry H. Richardson. Sullivan mentions this structure in "The Autobiography of an Idea" (1924, p. 188) as practically the only building that had impressed him. The project was rejected as too costly and returned to Sullivan for revision. He refused, however, to execute the required changes, so the contract was turned over to William C. Jones, a church-builder from Chicago. These plans were finally revised without compensation by Elmslie, who fortunately retained Sullivan's original concept.

Grundriß.
Main floor plan.

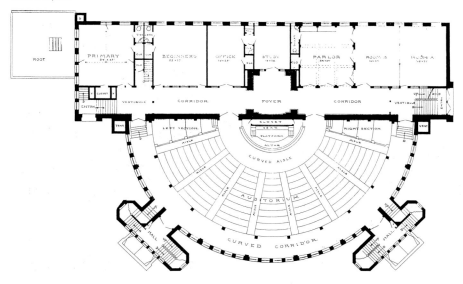

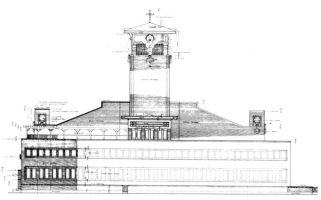

Nordfassade und Ansicht der St. Paul's Church.
North elevation and general view of St. Paul's Church.

Links: Turm der Brattle Square Church, Boston, 1870–1872.
Left: Tower of the Brattle Square Church, Boston, 1870–1872.

Haus Bennett   1911–1913

Owatonna, Minnesota, Projekt

Der Bankier Carl Bennett von der National Farmers' Bank in Owatonna engagierte Sullivan auch als Architekten für sein Wohnhaus. Abermals zeigte dieser jedoch wenig Gespür für familiär-bürgerliche Ansprüche und verlor schließlich den Auftrag. Vom Ungeschick Sullivans profitierten Elmslie & Purcell, die den Auftrag 1914 übernahmen, jedoch ebenfalls nie ausführen konnten. An Sullivans Konzeption erinnerte sich Mrs. Bennett 1957 wie folgt: «Mr. Sullivan's conception of our home was that it should be like a flower opening its petals toward the sun and so he made at the south side of the house mostly windows, and the north wall had no windows as I remember it.» Das Haus sollte mit drei verschiedenen Materialien verkleidet werden, die sich wie ein Kommentar zur dahinterliegenden Nutzung lesen lassen. Die Holzpaneele des Piano Nobile mit ihren sichtbaren Befestigungsbolzen erinnern an die Gestaltung des Wiener Postsparkassenamts (1903–1910) von Otto Wagner.

Bennett Residence   1911–1913

Owatonna, Minnesota; project

The banker Carl Bennett, from the National Farmer's Bank in Owatonna, engaged Sullivan as the architect for his residence. However, due to Sullivan's lack of sensitivity for middle-class family values, he eventually lost the commission. Benefitting from this clumsiness, Elmslie & Purcell were asked to take over the contract in 1914. Their design was also never executed. Mrs. Bennett recalled Sullivan's concept behind his design: "Mr. Sulivan's conception of our home was that it should be like a flower opening its petals toward the sun and so he made at the south side of the house mostly windows, and the north wall had no windows as I remember it." The exterior of the house was to be faced with three different materials that corresponded with the different usages of space behind the façade. The visible bolts on the wooden panels of the piano nobile are reminiscent of the style of Otto Wagner's Post Office Savings Bank in Vienna (1903–1910).

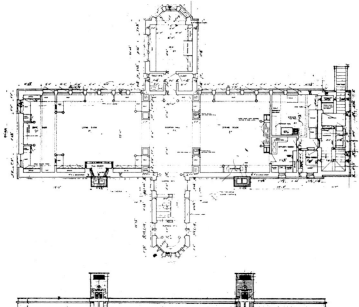

Grundriß des Wohngeschosses.
Main floor plan.

Nordfassade.
North elevation.

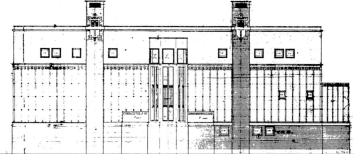

Adams Building   1913

Nordwestecke Moore und State Streets, Algona, Iowa

Ähnlich wie die Bankgebäude besteht das Geschäftshaus des Immobilienhändlers Henry C. Adams aus einem einzigen Raum. Programmatisch kommen bei diesem bescheidenen Bau die gestalterischen Prinzipien zum Tragen: der einfache Kubus, Zusammenfassung der Öffnungen, Gliederung durch Ornamente statt durch tektonische Struktur, wodurch die Fassade zu einer Art Bilderrahmen wird. Für die Erweiterung wurde zuerst Parker N. Berry, der als Angestellter Sullivans die Projektpläne der ersten Etappe gezeichnet hatte, 1920 nochmals Sullivan zugezogen, doch beide Vorschläge blieben unausgeführt.

Adams Building   1913

Northwest corner of Moore and State Streets, Algona, Iowa

The office building of the real-estate agent, Henry C. Adams, like the bank buildings, consists of one large space. The stylistic principles of this modest building are expressed programmatically: the simple cuboid from, the arrangement of openings into a unit, the organisation through ornament rather than tectonic structure, all serve to make the façade a kind of picture frame. Parker N. Berry, who had drawn up the project plans for the first phase as an employee of Sullivan, was initially engaged for the extension; however, Sullivan was again consulted later (1920). Neither draft was executed.

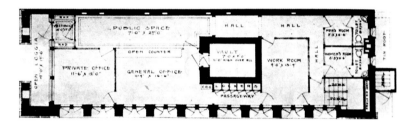

Grundriß und Ansicht.
Floor plan and general view.

Merchants National Bank   1913/14

Nordwestecke 4th und Broad Streets, Grinnell, Ohio

Sullivan entwarf das Projekt innerhalb von drei Tagen vor Ort und besprach die Skizzen anschließend mit den Auftraggebern. Er bezeichnete sein Bankgebäude selbst als «jewel box». Auffällige Ornamente finden sich vor allem auf der Frontseite. Die Verschränkung geometrischer Figuren hat Sullivan immer schon interessiert, hier finden sie jedoch eine spezifische ikonographische Rechtfertigung. Die «heftig ineinandergepreßten Rahmenformen» (Robert Venturi 1966, S. 65) aus Tonplatten verhalten sich zur runden Öffnung wie der Verschlußmechanismus einer Kamera zur Optik. Sie können auch als symbolische Darstellung der Verriegelungsvorrichtung der Tresortür gedeutet werden, die Sullivan hier wie anderswo gut sichtbar auf der Achse des Eingangs inszenierte.

Merchants National Bank   1913/14

Northwest corner of 4th and Broad Streets, Grinnell, Ohio

Sullivan sketched this design in three days on the spot. He himself described this bank building as the "jewel box". Notable is the striking ornament, particularly on the front face of the bank. Sullivan's particular penchant for crisscrossing geometric forms finally finds a specific iconographic justification in this building. The "violently superimposed frames" (Robert Venturi 1966, p. 65) of terra-cotta tiles relate to the round opening as a shutter mechanism in a camera relates to the lens. Furthermore, they can be interpreted as symbolic representations of the locking mechanism on the vault, centered here as elsewhere exactly on the main axis, plainly visible and directly opposite the entrance.

Grundrisse und Längsschnitt.
Floor plans and longitudinal section.

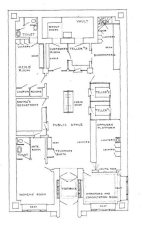
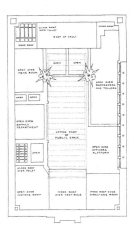

Sullivans Skizze eines Ornaments, Bleistift, 2. April 1902.
Ornamental design by Sullivan, pencil, April 2nd 1902.

Photo des Haupteingangs von Henry Fuermann.
Photo of the main entrance by Henry Fuermann.

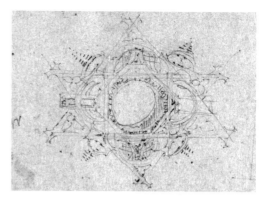

148

Photo von Henry Fuermann.
Photo by Henry Fuermann.

Schalterhalle und Tresortüre, Photos von Henry Fuermann.
Banking lobby and vault door, photos by Henry Fuermann.

John D. Van Allen & Sons-Warenhaus   1913–1915

Nordwestecke 5th Avenue und 2nd Street, Clinton, Iowa
Sullivan griff für dieses Projekt auf Gestaltungsmittel sei-
ner früheren Warenhäuser (Schlesinger & Mayer, Gage
Brothers) zurück: edle Materialien, welche die großen
Glasflächen der Schaufenster fassen, horizontale Fenster-
bänder in den Obergeschossen und drei vorgeblendete
Stengel mit ornamentalen Blüten an der Hauptfassade.
Zur Komposition der Fassade äußerte er sich in einem
Brief vom 23. März 1911: «This effect is based on the
plain surfaces, the elegance of chaste lines and harmonious proportions.» Die meisten Kritiker bekunden Mühe
mit den aufgesetzten Ornamenten, doch besitzen sie die
gleiche optische Funktion wie die Doppel-T-Träger an den
Hochhausfassaden von Mies van der Rohe. Die Stengel
fassen die Geschosse in vertikaler Hinsicht zusammen. Sie
werden dabei durch die asymmetrische Sprossenteilung
der angrenzenden Fenster unterstützt (Jordy 1986,
S. 140). Die Joche entlang der Hauptfassade sind ungleich
und verbreitern sich sukzessive gegen die Gebäudeecke
hin.

John D. Van Allen & Sons Store   1913–1915

Northwest corner of 5th Avenue and 2nd Street, Clinton,
Iowa
Sullivan utilized stylistic elements from his earlier department stores (Schlesinger & Mayer, Gage Brothers) for this
project: fine materials framing the large glass surfaces of
the display-windows; horizontal bands of windows in the
upper floors interrupted by three slender mullions applied
to the main façade terminating in bursts of ornamental
foliage. In a letter dated March 23, 1911, Sullivan com-
mented on the design of the façade: "This effect is based
on the plain surfaces, the elegance of the chaste lines and
harmonious proportions." Although most critics express
difficulty with the manner in which the ornament is "stuck
onto" the façade, it does seem to function optically like
the double-T-girders on the skyscraper façades of Mies
van der Rohe. The piers as well as the asymmetrical seg-
mentation of the adjacent windows serve to unite the
façade vertically (Jordy, 1986, p. 140). The bays along the
main façade, which are unequal in size, get successively
wider toward the corners of the building.

Während der Bauarbeiten.
Under construction.

Ludwig Mies van der Rohe:
Commonwealth Promenade
Apartements, Chicago,
1953–1956, Ecke und Schnitt.
Ludwig Mies van der Rohe:
Commonwealth Promenade
Apartements, Chicago,
1953–1956, corner and
section.

Photo von Richard Nickel.
Photo by Richard Nickel.

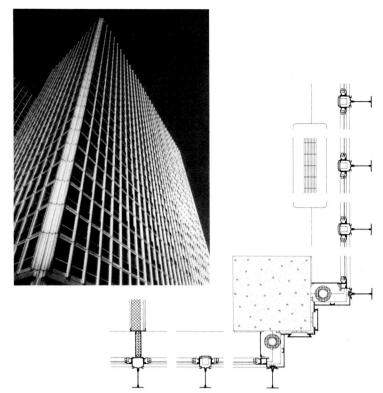

Home Building Association Bank   1914/15

Nordwestecke West Main und North 3rd Streets, Newark, Ohio

Der Bau entstand im Zusammenhang mit einer Kampagne zur Verschönerung der Stadt (Weingarden 1987, S. 108). Das kleine Grundstück zwang Sullivan, die Geschäftsräume auf insgesamt drei Geschosse (inklusive Keller) zu verteilen. Die Tragstruktur besteht aus einem Eisenskelett. Die Straßenfassaden wurden mit grünlich-grauen Tontafeln verkleidet. Die Ornamente bilden Rahmen, die entweder die Kontur des Volumens oder die Ränder der Öffnungen nachzeichnen. Obwohl formal sehr verschieden von den andern Bankgebäuden, ist auch hier die Artikulation von Hülle und Inhalt durch die Gestaltung der vermittelnden Öffnungen wesentlich. Das farbige Mosaik über dem Eingang gestaltete Louis Millet.

Home Building Association Bank   1914/15

Northwest corner of West Main and North 3rd Streets, Newark, Ohio

The building was erected as part of a campaign to beautify the city (Weingarden, 1987, p. 108). The small dimensions of the lot forced Sullivan to design a three-story structure (including a basement designed for office space). The structure consisted of a steel skeleton-frame construction. The street front façades were covered with greenish-gray terra-cotta slabs. An ornamental border follows the outline of the building and the edges of the openings. This building is formally quite different from the other bank buildings Sullivan designed. However, the articulation of the exterior and interior by means of the arrangement of the openings which connect them is also here essential. The colorful mosaic over the entrance was designed by Louis Millet.

Photo von Henry Fuermann.
Photo by Henry Fuermann.

Grundriß.
Floor plan.

Photo von Henry Fuermann.
Photo by Henry Fuermann.

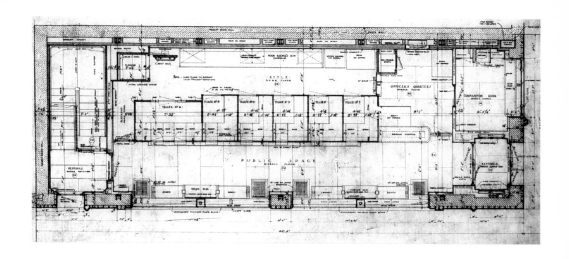

Peoples Savings & Loan Association Bank 1917/18

Südostecke Court Street und Ohio Avenue, Sidney, Ohio
Über Sullivans Vorgehen berichtet der damalige Bankpräsident W. H. Wagner: «Sullivan retired to the opposite corner, sat on a curbstone for the better part of two whole days, smoking innumerable cigarettes. Then at the end of that time, he announced to the directors that the design was made – in his head. He proceeded to rapidly draw a sketch for them, and announced an estimate of the cost. One of the directors was somewhat disturbed by the unfamiliarity of the style, and suggested that he rather fancied some classic columns and pilasters for the facade. Sullivan very brusquely rolled up his sketch and started to depart, saying that the directors could get a thousand architects to design a classic bank but only one to design this kind of bank, and that as far as he was concerned, it was one or the other.» Die großen Fenster der Straßenfassaden ruhen auf einem durchlaufenden Gesims. Sie werden durch stabförmige Rahmen aus gebranntem Ton gefaßt, die wie durch broschenartige Tafeln an die Backsteinwand geheftet zu sein scheinen. «Here character ends and caricature begins», bemerkt Hugh Morrison dazu, hält das Bauwerk insgesamt jedoch trotzdem, in Übereinstimmung mit Sullivan übrigens, für das beste aller Bankgebäude (Morrison 1935, S. 222). Die Schalterhalle war mit einer gut funktionierenden Klimaanlage versehen: Die verbrauchte Luft wurde bei den vier Pylonen in den Ecken der Schalterhalle abgesogen. Nachdem Sullivan herausgefunden hatte, daß der Tresor während der Geschäftszeiten normalerweise offenstand, verschob er den Zugang zum Tresor aus der Mittelachse, so daß nun die imposante Tresortür in geöffneter Position dem Eingang gegenüber zu liegen kam. Louis N. Berry zeichnete die Ausführungspläne, während Louis Millet wiederum für die Mosaikfelder an den Fassaden zuständig war.

Peoples Savings & Loan Association Bank 1917/18

Southwest corner of Court Street and Ohio Avenue, Sidney, Ohio
W. H. Wagner, the bank president at the time, describes the manner in which Sullivan approached his work: "Sullivan retired to the opposite corner, sat on a curbstone for the better part of two whole days, smoking innumerable cigarettes. At the end of this time, he announced to the directors that the design was made – in his head. He proceeded to draw a rapid sketch for them, and announced an estimate of the cost. One of the directors was somewhat disturbed by the unfamiliarity of the style, and suggested that he rather fancied some classic columns and pilasters for the façade. Sullivan very brusquely rolled up his sketch and started to depart, saying that the directors could get a thousand architects to design a classic bank but only one to design this kind of bank, and that as far as he was concerned, it was either one or the other." The large side windows facing the street rest on a continuous sill. They are framed by rod-shaped terra-cotta mullions which seem to be "pinned" to the brick façade by brooch-like escutcheons. Although Hugh Morrison (in accord with Sullivan) considers this building to be the finest of all bank buildings, he nevertheless made the following remark, "Here character ends and caricature begins" (Morrison, 1935, p. 222). The main lobby was equipped with an excellent ventilation system: the used air was circulated through air outlets in the four pylons in the corners of the hall. After Sullivan had found out that the vault would normally remain open during banking hours, he shifted the door to the vault off-center, in order to bring the imposing vault door back in line with the central axis when open. Louis N. Berry drafted the plans, and Louis Millet again executed the façade mosaics.

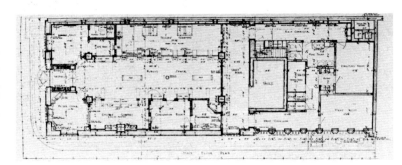

Grundriß.
Floor plan.

Rechte Seite / *right page*:
Photos von Henry Fuermann.
Photos by Henry Fuermann.

Farmers & Merchants Union Bank   1919/20

Nordwestecke James und Dickson Streets, Columbus, Wisconsin

In Sullivans letzter Bank sind nochmals alle wichtigen Merkmale seiner Bankgebäude zusammengefaßt: die Lage an einer prominenten Straßenkreuzung einer Kleinstadt, die große Schalterhalle, eingehüllt in Fassaden aus rauhem Backstein («tapestry brick or oriental brick»). Wiederum setzte Sullivan die Gestaltungsmittel auf unkonventionelle Weise ein: der übertrieben dimensionierte Sturz auf der Frontseite wird zur Werbetafel; die Strebepfeiler der Längsfassade leiten keine Gewölbelasten ab, sondern rahmen bloß eine Folge von Bogenfenstern; diese wiederum sind als Nischen in die Fassade eingelassen und werden über die Kämpferzone durch einen dekorierten Schild aus Tonplatten abgeschlossen. Da Sullivan 1918 die Räume im Auditorium Building hatte aufgeben müssen, entstand das Projekt mit Hilfe von William C. Presto in seinem neuen Büro an 1800 Prairie Avenue.

Farmers & Merchants Union Bank   1919/20

Northwest corner of James and Dickson Streets; Columbus, Wisconsin

All the important features of Sullivan's bank buildings are again integrated in his last bank design: the building site was on a prominent intersection of a small American town in the Midwest; the large lobby was wrapped in façades of rough brick ("tapestry brick or oriental brick"). Again Sullivan employs traditional stylistic features in an unconventional way: the over-sized lintel on the front façade containing the name of the bank becomes a billboard; the pier buttresses on the side façade do not support the load of a vault, they only serve to frame a series of arched windows; these windows are recessed into the façade like niches topped off above the imposts by a decorated band of terra-cotta spandrels. As Sullivan was forced to give up his offices in the Auditorium Building in 1918, this project was executed in his new office on 1800 Prairie Avenue with the help of William C. Presto.

Rechte Seite / *right page*:
Photos von Henry Fuermann.
Photos by Henry Fuermann.

Sullivans Entwürfe der Frontfassade vom 15. Februar 1919 (links), 1. März 1919 (Mitte) und 31. März 1919 (rechts, gebaute Variante).
Sullivan's drawings of the front elevation from February 15th 1919 (left), March 1st 1919 (middle) and March 31st 1919 (right, final project).

 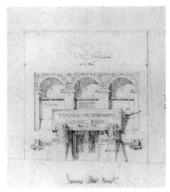 

Photos von Henry Fuermann.
Photos by Henry Fuermann.

Musikgeschäft Krause (Music Store)   1922

4611 Lincoln Avenue, Chicago

William C. Presto bot seinem früheren Chef an, bei seinem ersten eigenen Auftrag die Gestaltung der Fassade zu übernehmen. Es ist der autonome Status der Dekoration, der für Sullivan eine solche Arbeitsteilung möglich machte und zugleich die Beziehung zwischen innen und außen, Funktion und Form neu bestimmte. Edison-Birnen rahmen das Schaufenster.

Krause Music Store   1922

4611 Lincoln Avenue, Chicago

William C. Presto had offered his former boss the façade design on the first commission he received on his own. The autonomous status of the decoration enabled Sullivan to make this kind of "division of labor" and at the same time redefine the relationship between inside and outside, function and form. The lower display-window is framed by Edison light bulbs.

Photo von Henry Fuermann.
Photo by Henry Fuermann.

«Ein System arechitektonischer Ornamentik»
1924

Sullivan wurde, da er ohne Bauaufträge war, von einigen Freunden ermutigt, neben «The Autobiography of an Idea» auch ein Werk über seine Theorie der Ornamentik zu verfassen. «A System of Architectural Ornament According with a Philosophy of Man's Power» erschien 1924, kurz nach seinem Tode. Sullivan gründete das System der Ornamentierung weder auf konstruktive noch funktionelle Voraussetzungen. Ornamente sind stets etwas Hinzugefügtes, das eigenen Gesetzen gehorcht, jedoch kein beliebiger Zuckerguß ist. Gemäß Sullivans Parallelismusbegriff sollen sie mit andern Sachverhalten wie Struktur, Bedeutung und Funktion korrespondieren. In diesem Sinne auch ersetzt Sullivan die euklidische Geometrie durch eine organische, wonach der «Impuls aus dem Keim» überall «Ausdruck in der Form» (Tafel 9) sucht: «Daher kann man den Keim als einen Energiequell betrachten, der im Laufe der Suche nach seiner endgültigen, charakteristischen Form – dem Ausdruck seiner Identität – selbständig sekundäre Energiezentren bildet» (Sullivan 1924, Tafel 4).

"A System of Architectural Ornament"
1924

Due to the lack of building commissions, Sullivan was encouraged by some of his friends to write another work besides "The Autobiography of an Idea", illustrating his theory of architectural ornament. "A System of Architectural Ornament According with a Philosophy of Man's Power" was published in 1924 shortly after his death. Sullivan bases his system of ornament neither on structural nor on functional criteria. Ornament is always something "added on"; nevertheless it is governed by its own set of laws. It is not an arbitrary icing. According to Sullivan's concept of parallelism, ornament should correspond to other aspects of architecture, such as structure, significance and function. In this way, Sullivan replaces euclidean geometry by an organic one, whereby "energy from the seed-germ" strives for "expression in form" (Plate 9): "The seed-germ may thus be considered also as a container of energy, forming of its own will sub-centers of energy in the course of its functioning development toward the finality of its characteristic form – the expression of its identity" (Sullivan, 1924, Plate 4).

Sullivans Zeichnung «Fließender Parallelismus (nicht-euklidisch)», Tafel 10 aus «A System of Architectural Ornament» (1924).
Sullivan's drawing «Fluent Parallelism (non-euclidian)», plate 10 of «A System of Architectural Ornament» (1924).

Sullivans Logo («Denkt an den Keim»).
Sullivan's Logo.

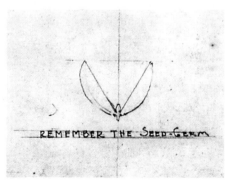

REMEMBER THE SEED-GERM

Lebensabriß
Biographical Notes

Diese Kurzbiographie stützt sich auf Robert Twomblys Chronologie in: de Wit 1986, Seiten 212–214.

List based on Robert Twombly's Chronology in: de Wit 1986, pages 212–214.

1856

3. September: Louis Henry Sullivan wird in Boston, Massachusetts, geboren.

1856

September 3: Louis Henry Sullivan born in Boston, Massachusetts.

1870

Juni: Abschluß der Rice Grammar School in Boston.

1870

June: graduates from Rice Grammar School, Boston.

1870–1872

Besuch der English High School in Boston.

1870–1872

Attends English High School, Boston.

1872

Oktober: Eintritt in das Massachusetts Institute of Technology (MIT), Abteilung für Bauen und Architektur.

1872

October: enters Massachusetts Institute of Technology (MIT), Building and Architecture Departement.

1873

Juni: Sullivan verläßt das MIT und tritt in die Firma Furness & Hewitt in Philadelphia ein. – November: Er verläßt Furness & Hewitt und beginnt im Büro von William Le Baron Jenney in Chicago zu arbeiten.

1873

June: leaves MIT, joins the firm of Furness & Hewitt in Philadelphia. – November: leaves Furness & Hewitt, enters William Le Baron Jenney's office in Chicago.

1874

10. Juli: Sullivan schifft sich in New York nach Liverpool ein. – August: Er reist nach Paris und wohnt an der rue Racine Nr. 17. – 22. Oktober: Wird an der École des Beaux-Arts in Paris als Architekturstudent aufgenommen.

1874

July 10: sails from New York for Liverpool. – August: arrives in Paris, lives at 17 rue Racine. – October 22: admitted to the École des Beaux-Arts, Paris, as a student in architecture.

1875

April–Mai: Reist durch Südfrankreich, Norditalien und nach Rom. – 24. Mai: Trifft von Liverpool her kommend in New York ein und beginnt als freischaffender Entwerfer in Chicago zu arbeiten.

1875

April–May: tours southern France, northern Italy, Rome. May 24: arrives in New York from Liverpool, begins work as a free-lance designer/draftsman in Chicago.

1879

Im Rahmen seiner freischaffenden Tätigkeit arbeitet Sullivan auch für «Dankmar Adler, Architect», Chicago.

1879

Free lancing includes work for "Dankmar Adler, Architect", Chicago.

1881

Sullivan wird Partner bei «Dankmar Adler & Company».

1881

Becomes partner in "Dankmar Adler & Company".

1883

1. Mai: Wird gleichberechtigter Partner im Architekturbüro «Adler & Sullivan». – 17. November: Gründungsmitglied der Western Association of Architects.

1883

May 1: Becomes principal in "Adler & Sullivan". – November 17: founding member of the Western Association of Architects.

1885

Januar: Gründungsmitglied der Illinois State Association of Architects.

1887

21. Oktober: Sullivan wird zum Mitglied des American Institute of Architects gewählt.

1888

Februar: Frank Lloyd Wright tritt in das Büro «Adler & Sullivan» ein.

1889

9. April: Vortrag von «Style» im Chicago Architectural Sketch Club. – Herbst: Das Büro «Adler & Sullivan» zieht um in den Auditorium Tower.

1893

Frühling: Frank Lloyd Wright verläßt «Adler & Sullivan». – 5. August: Vortrag von «Polychromatic Treatment of Architecture» vor dem World Congress of Architects an der Weltausstellung in Chicago.

1894–1897

Vorstandsmitglied des American Institute of Architects.

1895

11. Juli: Dankmar Adler zieht sich von seiner Tätigkeit als Architekt zurück, was die Partnerschaft «Adler & Sullivan» beendet.

1895/96

Als Vorstandsmitglied des American Institute of Architects ist Sullivan im Hauptausschuß tätig.

1899

3. Juni: Vortrag «The modern Phase of Architecture» an der Gründungsversammlung der Architectural League of America in Cleveland. – 1. Juli: Louis Henry Sullivan heiratet Mary Azona Hattabaugh in der St. Paul's Reformed Episcopal Church in Chicago.

1900

Juni: Vortrag «The Young Man in Architecture» an der zweiten Versammlung der Architectural League of America in Chicago.

1901/02

Vom 16. Februar 1901 bis zum 8. Februar 1902: «Kindergarten chats» wird in 52 Fortsetzungen in Interstate Architect & Builder veröffentlicht.

1902

30. Mai: Vortrag «Education» an der vierten Versammlung der Architectural League of America in Toronto.

1905

Dezember: Sullivan bewirbt sich ohne Erfolg um einen Lehrauftrag an der Michigan School of Architecture.

1885

January: founding member of the Illinois State Association of Architects.

1887

October 21: elected fellow of the American Institute of Architects.

1888

February: Frank Lloyd Wright enters Adler & Sullivan's office.

1889

April 9: "Style" read to Chicago Architectural Sketch Club. – Fall: "Adler & Sullivan" move to Auditorium Tower office.

1893

Spring: Frank Lloyd Wright leaves "Adler & Sullivan". – August 5: "Polychromatic Treatment of Architecture" read to World Congress of Architects, Chicago World's Fair.

1894–1897

Member of Board of Directors, American Institute of Architects.

1895

July 11: Dankmar Adler leaves architectural profession terminating the "Adler & Sullivan" partnership.

1895/96

Serves on executive committee, Board of Directors, American Institute of Architects.

1899

June 3: "The modern Phase of Architecture" read to founding convention of the Architectural League of America, Cleveland. – July 1: marries Mary Azona Hattabaugh at St. Paul's Reformed Episcopal Church, Chicago.

1900

June: "The Young Man in Architecture" read to second Architectural League of America convention, Chicago.

1901/02

February 16, 1901 – February 8, 1902: "Kindergarten chats" published in 52 instalments of Interstate Architect & Builder.

1902

May 30: "Education" read to fourth Architectural League of America convention, Toronto.

1905

December: fails to secure lectureship at University of Michigan School of Architecture.

1908

Herbst: Beendigt sein Manuskript «Democracy: A Man-Search», an dem er seit 1905 unter dem Titel «Natural Thinking: A Study in Democracy» gearbeitet hat.

1909

29. November: Sullivans persönliche Habe und der geschäftliche Besitz gelangen im Auktionssaal der Williams, Barker & Severns Company in Chicago zur Versteigerung. – 6. Dezember: Mary Sullivan verläßt ihren Ehemann.

1910

Frühling: Sullivan verkauft seinen Landsitz in Ocean Springs.

1916/17?

Scheidung von Mary und Louis Sullivan.

1918

Sullivan bemüht sich um eine Stelle als Staatsbeamter. – Februar: Kann die Miete seines Büros im Auditorium Tower nicht mehr bezahlen und zieht in zwei Räume in der zweiten Etage desselben Gebäudes um. – Mai: Kann die Mietkosten nicht aufbringen und gibt sein Büro im Auditorium Building auf. – Oktober: Neues Büro an der Prairie Avenue 1808.

1921

November: Neues Büro an der Prairie Avenue 1701.

1922/23

Vom Juni 1922 bis zum September 1923: In der Zeitschrift The American Institute of Architects Journal wird «The Autobiography of an Idea» in fünfzehn Fortsetzungen veröffentlicht.

1924

14. April: Louis Henry Sullivan stirbt in seinem Zimmer im Warner-Hotel an einem Nierenleiden und Myokarditis. – 16. April: Beisetzung im Graceland-Friedhof in Chicago.

1908

Fall: completes manuscript of "Democracy: A Man-Search", written since 1905 under the title "Natural Thinking: A Study in Democracy".

1909

November 29: personal and professional possessions sold at Williams, Barker & Severns Company auction showroom, Chicago. – December 6: Mary Sullivan leaves her husband.

1910

Spring: sells Ocean Springs land.

1916/17?

Mary and Louis Sullivan divorce.

1918

Looks for civil service job with federal government. – February: unable to pay rent, leaves Auditorium Tower office for two rooms at the second floor of the same building. – May: unable to pay rent, gives up the Auditorium Building office. – October: new office at 1808 Prairie Avenue.

1921

November: new office at 1701 Prairie Avenue.

1922/23

June 1922–September 1923: publishes "The Autobiography of an Idea" in fifteen instalments of The American Institute of Architects Journal.

1924

April 14: Louis Henry Sullivan dies in his Warner Hotel room of kidney disease and myocarditis. – April 16: buried in Graceland Cemetery, Chicago.

Werkverzeichnis
Work Chronology

Die folgende Aufstellung basiert auf dem Verzeichnis von Robert Twombly, in Twombly 1986, Seiten 445–459.
Das +) bezeichnet noch bestehende Gebäude.
*Das *) kennzeichnet Bauten und Entwürfe, die im Katalogteil des vorliegenden Buches behandelt werden.*
Bei Gebäuden, die nicht für Chicago bestimmt waren, wird die entsprechende Stadt angeführt. Bei noch bestehenden Gebäuden ist der Straßenname genannt; weitere Angaben betreffen den gegenwärtigen Zustand.

Based on list by Robert Twombly, in Twombly 1986, pages 445–459.
+): Building still existing.
*): Building referred to in the catalogue.
For buildings outside Chicago, the city names are applied; for buildings still existing, the street names are applied. Further informations on actual condition.

Freiberuflicher Entwerfer / Free-lance designer
1876–1878
1. Chicago Avenue Church ("Moody's Tabernacle"), Innenraumgestaltung / interior decoration, für/for Johnston & Edelmann, architects.
2. Sinai Synagogue, Innenraumgestaltung / interior decoration, für/for Burling & Adler, Johnston & Edelmann, associated architects.

1879
3. *) Central Music Hall, Innenraumgestaltung / interior decoration, für/for Adler.

1880
4. *) John Borden Block, für/for Adler.
5. *) John Borden Residence, für/for Adler.
6. Grand Opera House, Innenraumgestaltung / interior decorations, für/for Adler.

1881
7. *) Max M. Rothschild Building, für/for Adler.

Partner in "Adler & Company"
8. *) John M. Brunswick & Julius Balke Factory.
9. Levi Rosenfeld Flats.
10. +)*) Jewelers' Building, 15–19 South Wabash Avenue, Chicago, (Ladenfront verändert / shop front altered).

11. *) Revell Building.
12. Academy of Music, Kalamazoo, Michigan.

1882
13. *) John M. Brunswick & Julius Balke Warehouse.
14. Frankenthal Building.
15. Hammond Library.
16. Hooley's Theater Umbau/remodeling.
17. Sigmund Hyman Residence.
18. Charles F. Kimball Residence.
19. Henry Leopold Residence.
20. Levi Rosenfeld Flats and Store.
21. Max M. Rosenfeld Flats.
22. Marx Wineman Residence.

1883
23. F. L. Brand Store and Flats.

"Adler & Sullivan"
24. Aurora Watch Company, Aurora, Illinois.
25. *) John M. Brunswick & Julius Balke lumber-drying plant, Entwurf/project.
26. +)*) Ann Halsted Residence, 440 West Beldon Street, Chicago.
27. +) Ferdinand & William Kauffmann Store and Flats,

2310–2314 Lincoln Avenue, Chicago (2316 Lincoln Avenue abgerissen/demolished).

28. Frank A. Kennedy Bakery (1883–1884).
29. Richard Knisely Store and Flats.
30. J. H. McVicker's Theater, Entwurf/project.
31. Max M. Rothschild Flats.
32. Reuben Rubel Store and Flats.
33. Schoolhouse Marengo, Illinois, Umbau/remodeling.
34. *) Charles H. Schwab Residence.
35. Scoville & Towne Factory, Entwurf/project.
36. *) Morris Selz Residence.

1884

37. Martin Barbe Residence.
38. Solomon Blumenfeld Flats.
39. Lewis E. Frank Residence.
40. +)*) Ann Halsted Flats, 1826–34 Lincoln Park West, Chicago.
41. J. H. Haverly Theater Umbau/remodeling.
42. Interstate Exposition Building, teilweiser Umbau der Innenräume für die / partial interior remodeling for Democratic National Convention.
43. Richard Knisely Factory.
44. Lakeside Clubhouse, Entwurf/project.
45. Manhattan Bank, New York City, Lifteinbau / bronce elevator car.
46. Mandel Brothers Stable.
47. +) Leon Mannheimer Residence, 2147 North Cleveland Street, Chicago.
48. Max M. Rothschild Flats.
49. Reuben Rubel Residence.
50. *) Martin A. Ryerson Building.
51. Leopold Schlesinger Residence.
52. B. & S. Schoeneman Factory.
53. Sinai Synagogue, Innenumbau und Instandsetzung /interior remodeling and repairs.
54. Abraham Strauss Residence.
55. Leopold Strauss Residence.
56. *) A. F. Troescher Building.

1885

57. Dankmar Adler Residence.
58. *) Chicago Opera Festival, Innenumbau des / interior remodeling of the Interstate Exposition Building.
59. Chiltenham Improvement Company Pavilion.
60. Eli B. Felsenthal Residence.
61. +)*) Ann Halsted Flats, Ergänzung zu / addition to entry 40.
62. Fanny Kohn Residence.

63. Abraham Kuh Residence.
64. Benjamin Lindauer Residence.
65. *) J. H. McVicker's Theater Umbau/remodeling.
66. Walter L. Peck Double Residence.
67. J. M. Scoville Factory, (Anbauten und Änderungen / additions and alterations).
68. M. C. Stearns Residence.
69. Henry Stern Residence.
70. Samuel Stern Residence.
71. George Watson Warehouse Anbau/addition.
72. Wright & Lawther Factory Anbau/addition.
73. Zion Temple.

1886

74. Arthur Block, Umbau zu Wohnungen / conversion to flats.
75. +)*) Auditorium Building, Congress Street, Michigan and Wabash Avenues, Chicago.
76. Chicago Opera House, Auditorium Umbau / remodeling.
77. Richard T. Crane Factory.
78. +) Joseph Deimal Residence, 3141 Calumet Avenue, (stark verändert / considerably altered).
79. +) Dessenberg Building, 251 East Michigan Avenue, Kalamazoo, Michigan.
80. +) Mathilde Eliel Residence, 4122 Ellis Avenue, Chicago.
81. Levi A. Eliel Residence.
82. Hugo Goodman Residence.
83. Hannah Horner Residence.
84. Illinois Central Railroad Station 39th Street.
85. F. M. Jones Residence.
86. Milwaukee Exposition Building, Innenumbau / interior remodeling.
87. Edward G. Pauling Flats.
88. Walter and Clarence Peck Warehouse.
89. Martin A. Ryerson Charities Trust Building.
90. Solomon Residence, Entwurf/project.
91. West Chicago Clubhouse.

1887

92. Chicago Nursery & Half Orphan Asylum.
93. Rudolph Deimal Residence, Entwurf/project.
94. Rudolph Deimal & Bros. Factory and Warehouse.
95. +)*) Wirt Dexter Building, 630 South Wabash Avenue, Chicago, (Giebel entfernt / pediment removed).
96. John Krantz Building, Umbau/remodeling.
97. Mary M. Lively Residence.

98. Adolph Loeb Factory.

99. *) Martin A. Ryerson Building, Entwurf/project.

100. +)*) Martin A. Ryerson Tomb, Graceland Cemetery, Chicago.

101. B. & S. Schoeneman Factory, Anbau/addition.

102. Selz, Schwab Factory.

103. Springer Building, Umbau/remodeling

104. *) Standard Club House.

1888

105. Victor Falkenau Flats.

106. Patrick Farrell Flats and Barn, Entwurf/project.

107. Patrick Farrell Residence, Entwurf/project.

108. +) George M. Harvey Residence, 600 West Stratford Place, Chicago (innen und außen stark verändert / extensively remodeled inside and out).

109. Illinois Central Railroad Station 43rd Street.

110. Lazarus Silverman Building, Anbau/addition.

111. *) James H. Walker Warehouse.

1889

112. Eliphalet W. Blachford Warehouse.

113. Milan C. Bullock Factory.

114. +) Carnegie Hall, 47th Street, New York City, Beratung/consultants 1889–1890.

115. Wirt Dexter Residence, Umbauentwurf / project for alterations.

116. Eli B. Felsenthal Factory.

117. Ira Heath Residence, Entwurf/project.

118. Inter-Ocean Building, Zusätze und Änderungen / additions and alterations.

119. +)*) Kehilath Anshe Ma'ariv Synagogue, 33th Street and Indiana Avenue, Chicago.

120. *) Opera House Block, Pueblo, Colorado.

121. Polish and Russian Manual Training School.

1890

122. James C. Berry Residence, Entwurf/project.

123. +)*) James Charnley Cottage, Ocean Boulevard, Ocean Springs, Mississippi (seitliche Vorhallen hinzugefügt / side porches added).

124. Chicago Cold Storage Exchange Warehouse.

125. Richard T. Crane Factory.

126. *) Dooly Block, Salt Lake City, Utah.

127. +)*) Carrie Elizabeth Getty Tomb, Graceland Cemetery, Chicago.

128. Grand Opera House, Milwaukee, Wisconsin, Umbau/remodeling.

129. *) J. H. McVicker's Theater, Wiederaufbau/reconstruction.

130. *) Ontario Hotel, Salt Lake City, Utah, Entwurf/project.

131. Opera House Block, Seattle, Washington, Entwurf/project.

132. Schiller Building (1890–1892).

133. *) Schlesinger & Mayer Store, Anbauten und Veränderungen / additions and alterations.

134. +)*) Louis H. Sullivan Cottage, Ocean Boulevard, Ocean Springs, Mississippi (bis zur Unkenntlichkeit verändert / altered beyond recognition).

135. +)*) Wainwright Building, northwest corner of Seventh and Chestnut Streets, St. Louis, Missouri, umgebaut durch / remodeled by Hastings & Chivetta, Mitchell & Giurgola.

136. Wright, Hill & Co. Factory.

1891

137. C. H. Berry Residence.

138. *) John M. Brunswick & Julius Balke Factory, Anbau/addition.

139. +)*) James Charnley Residence, 1365 North Astor Street, Chicago, saniert durch / reconstructed by Skidmore Owings & Merrill.

140. Illinois Central Passenger Terminal, New Orleans, Louisiana.

141. Adolph and William Loeb Store and Flats.

142. Mercantile Club Building, St. Louis, Missouri, Entwurf/project.

143. Nashville Linoleum Company, Des Plaines, Illinois.

144. J. W. Oakley Warehouse.

145. *) Odd Fellows ("Fraternity") Temple Building, Entwurf/project.

146. *) Schlesinger & Maier Store, An- und Umbauten / additions and alterations.

147. Shone Ejector Company Factory.

148. Sinai Synagogue, Anbauten und Änderungen / additions and alterations.

149. +) Standard Elevator Company Factory, 1515 West 15th Street, Chicago.

150. *) Albert W. Sullivan Residence.

151. *) Transportation Building.

152. +)*) Charlotte Dickson Wainwright Tomb, Bellefontaine Cemetery, St. Louis, Missouri.

153. Walker & Oakley Tannery.

1892

154. *) William Mayer Warehouse.

155. Portland Building, St. Louis, Missouri, Entwurf/project.

156. *) Schlesinger & Mayer Store.
157. *) Standard Club, Anbauten und Änderungen / additions and alterations.
158. *) St. Nicholas Hotel, St. Louis, Missouri.
159. *) Nicht identifiziertes großes Gebäude / unidentified tall building.
160. +)*) Union Trust Building, northwest corner Seventh and Olive Streets, St. Louis, Missouri, (Ladenfront geändert / shop front altered).
161. *) Victoria Hotel, Chicago Heights, Illinois.

1893

162. J. T. Ball & Company Warehouse (1893–94).
163. +)*) Chicago Stock Exchange Building (Rekonstruktion von Eingang und Börsensaal im / reconstruction of entrance and trading room at The Art Institute of Chicago, Michigan Avenue at Adams Street, Chicago).
164. Eye & Ear Infirmary Anbau/addition.
165. First Regiment Armory Umbau/conversion to Trocadero Amusement Park.
166. Illinois Leather Company Tannery.
167. Mandel Brothers Stable.
168. Mandel Brothers Store, Sanierung und Anbau / reconstruction and addition.
169. Trust and Savings Building, St. Louis, Missouri, Entwurf/project
170. Wolf, Sayer & Heller Warehouse, Entwurf/addition.

1894

171. Hermann Braunstein Store and Flats.
172. Burnet House Hotel, Cincinnati, Ohio, Entwurf/project.
173. Chemical National Bank Building, St. Louis, Missouri, Entwurf/project, mutmaßliche Datierung/date is conjectural.
174. Chicago Dock Company Warehouse.
175. Levi A. Eliel Apartment Building, Entwurf/project.
176. +)*) Guaranty Building, southwest corner Pearl and Church Streets, Buffalo, New York.
177. Store Building, St. Louis, Missouri, Entwurf/project, mutmaßliche Datierung und unbekannter Auftraggeber/date is conjectural and client's name is unknown.

Selbständige Tätigkeit / Independent practice
1895

178. National Linseed Oil Company Cooper Shop.

1896

179. *) Schlesinger & Mayer Store, Anbauten und Entwurf / additions and project.

1897

180. +)*) Bayard (Condict) Building, 65 Bleecker Street, New York City, Ladenfront verändert / shop front altered.
181. Hippodrome, St. Louis, Missouri, Berater/consultant.

1898

182. County Club, Entwurf/project.
183 +)*) Gage Building, 18 South Michigan Avenue, Chicago.
184. A. W. Goodrich Residence, Harbor Springs, Michigan, Entwurf/project.
185. *) Schlesinger & Mayer Store, Entwurf/project.
186. +)*) Schlesinger & Mayer Store (now Carson Pirie Scott), Madison Street, Chicago, nine story building.

1899

187. Richard T. Crane Company, Foundry addition.
188. +) Alexander Euston & Company Factory, Kingsbury Street between Blackhawk and Eastman, Chicago.
189. +)*) Holy Trinity Cathedral, 1121 North Leavitt Street, Chicago.
190. Nettie F. McCormick Residence, Änderungen/alterations, Entwurf/project.

1901

191. Nettie F. McCormick Residence, Lake Forest, Illinois, Entwurf/project.
192. Presbyterian Hospital Women's Pavilion, Entwurf/project.
193. +) Virginia Hall, Tusculum College, Greeneville, Tennessee.
194. Ellis Wainwright Residence, St. Louis, Missouri, Entwurf/project.

1902

195. +) Euston & Company Factory, Kingsbury Street between Blackhawk and Eastman, Chicago.
196. Arthur Henry Lloyd Residence, Entwurf/project.
197. +)*) Schlesinger & Mayer Store (now Carson Pirie Scott), State and Madison Streets, Chicago, twelve story building.
198. *) Schlesinger & Mayer Store, Entwurf für zwanzig Stockwerke/twenty story project.

1903

199. Richard Crane Office Buildings, Bridgeport, Connecticut.
200. *) Schlesinger & Mayer Store, Änderungen/alterations.

1904

201. Crane Company Offices.
202. Office Building, project.
203. Theater façade, project.

1906

204. Eli B. Felsenthal Store and Flats.
205. +)*) National Farmers' Bank, Broadway and Cedar Street, Owatonna, Minnesota.

1907

206. *) Henry Babson Residence, Riverside, Illinois.
207. *) Island City Amusement Park, Philadelphia, Pennsylvania, Entwurf/project.

1908

208. Auditorium Building, Entwürfe zum Umbau als Hotel und Bürohaus / remodeling as Hotel and as Office Building, projects.
209. +)*) Josephine Crane Bradley Residence, 106 North Prospect Avenue, Madison, Wisconsin.

1909

210. +)*) Peoples Savings Bank, 3rd Avenue SW and 1st Street SW, Cedar Rapids, Iowa.

1910

211. +)*) St. Paul's Methodist Episcopal Church, 3rd Avenue SE and 14th Street SE, Cedar Rapids, Iowa.

1911

212. Carl K. Bennett Residence, Owatonna, Minnesota, 1911–1913, Entwürfe/projects.

1912

213. George Arndt Garage, Mt. Vernon, Ohio, Entwurf/project.

1913

214. +)*) Henry C. Adams Building, Moore and State Streets, Algona, Iowa.
215. +)*) John D. Van Allen & Sons Store, 5th Avenue South and 2nd Street, Clinton, Iowa.
216. +)*) Merchants National Bank, 4th Avenue and Broad Street, Grinnell, Iowa.
217. Museum, Entwurf/project.

1914

218. Bank, Enid, Oklahoma, Entwurf/project.
219. +)*) Home Building Association Bank, West Main and North 3rd Streets, Newark, Ohio (Eingang und Erdgeschoß verändert / entrance and ground floor altered).
220. +) Purdue State Bank, State and Vine Streets, West Lafayette, Indiana (Inneres vollständig verändert / interior completely altered).

1916

221. *) Henry C. Adams Building, Moore and State Streets, Algona, Iowa, Entwurf für Anbau / addition, project.
222. District High School, Owatonna, Minnesota, Entwurf/project.

1917

223. +)*) Peoples Savings & Loan Association Bank, Court Street and Ohio Avenue, Sidney, Ohio.

1919

224. +)*) Farmers & Merchants Union Bank, James Street and Broadway Avenue, Columbus, Wisconsin.
225. +) Bank, Manistique, Michigan, Umbau/remodeling.

1920

226. +) Denkmalsockel/pedestal for the Governor John Palmer Statue by Leonard Crunelle, Springfield, Illinois.

1921

227. Mrs. Arthur J. Eddy Tomb, Flint, Michigan, Entwurf/project.

1922

228. +)*) William P. Krause Music Store and Residence, 4611 Lincoln Avenue, Chicago.

Auswahlbibliographie
Selected Bibliography

Adler 1892 Dankmar Adler: The Chicago Auditorium. In: Architectural Record, New York, vol. 1, no. 4, April–June 1892, p. 415–434.

Andrew 1985 David S. Andrew: Louis Sullivan and the Polemics of Modern Architecture – The Present against the Past. Urbana, Chicago (University of Illinois Press) 1985.

Baumann 1901 Friedrich Baumann: Die Baukunst im Staate Illinois – Versuch einer geschichtlichen Darstellung. In: Deutsch-amerikanische Geschichtsblätter, Chicago, vol. 1, no. 1, 1901, p. 25–32.

Berlage 1912 Hendrik Peter Berlage: Neuere amerikanische Architektur. In: Schweizerische Bauzeitung, Zürich, vol. 60, September 14., 21. and 28., 1912, p. 148–150, 165–167, 178.

Blumenson 1977 John B. Blumenson: Identifying American Architecture – A Pictoral Guide to Styles and Terms, 1600–1945. Nashville 1977.

Brooks 1972 H. Allen Brooks: The Prairie School – Frank Lloyd Wright and his Midwest Contemporaries. New York (Norton) 1976 (first published 1972).

Chapman 1981 Linda L. Chapman (ed.): Louis H. Sullivan – Architectural Ornament Collection. Edwardsville (Southern Illinois University) 1981.

Condit 1964 Carl W. Condit: The Chicago School of Architecture – A History of Commercial and Public Building in the Chicago Area 1875–1925. Chicago and London (The University of Chicago Press) 1964.

Eaton 1972 Leonard K. Eaton: American Architecture comes of Age – European Reaction to H. H. Richardson and Louis Sullivan. Cambridge (Mass.)., London (MIT Press) 1972.

Giedion 1941 Sigfried Giedion: Space, Time and Architecture. Cambridge (Mass.) 1941 (dt. Übersetzung: Raum, Zeit, Architektur; Zürich, München 1976).

Gregersen 1990 Charles E. Gregersen: Dankmar Adler. His Theatres and Auditoriums. Athens (Ohio University Press) 1990.

Jordy 1986 William Jordy: The Tall Buildings. In: de Wit 1986, p. 65–157.

Kaufmann 1956 Edgar Kaufmann jr. (ed.): Louis Sullivan and the Architecture of Free Enterprise. Chicago (Art Institute) 1956.

Lavater 1775–1778 Johann Caspar Lavater: Physiognomische Fragmente – Zur Beförderung der Menschenkenntnis und Menschenliebe. 4 Bände. Leipzig, Winterthur 1775–1778 (Reprint: Zürich 1968; quoted english version: Essays on Physiognomy. 3 volumes. London 1804)

Levine 1977 Neil Levine: The Romantic Idea of Architectural Legibility; Henri Labrouste and the Néo Grec. In: Arthur Drexler (ed.): The Architecture of the École des Beaux-Arts. New York (The Museum of Modern Art) 1977, p. 324–416.

Loos 1908 Adolf Loos: Ornament und Verbrechen. 1908 (Reprint in: Adolf Loos: Sämtliche Schriften. 2 Bände. Wien, München, vol. 1, 1962, S. 276–287).

Menocal 1981 Narciso G. Menocal: Architecture as Nature – The Transcendentalist Idea of Louis Sullivan. Madison (The University of Wisconsin Press) 1981.

Millett 1985 Larry Millett: The Curve of the Arch – The Story of Louis Sullivan's Owatonna Bank. St. Paul (Minnesota Historical Society Press) 1985.

Morrison 1935 Hugh Morrison: Louis Sullivan. Prophet of Modern Architecture – New York (Norton) 1962 (first published 1935).

Mollmann 1989 Sarah C. Mollmann (ed.): Louis Sullivan in the Art Institute of Chicago – An Illustrated Catalogue of Collections. New York, London (Garland) 1989.

Mumford 1931 Lewis Mumford: The Brown Decades – A Study of the Arts in America, 1865–1895. New York (Dover) 1931.

Paul 1962 Sherman Paul: Louis Sullivan – An Architect in American Thought. Englewood Cliffs (N. Y.) (Prentice-Hall) 1962 (zitierte deutsche Übersetzung: Louis H. Sullivan – Ein amerikanischer Architekt und Denker. Berlin 1963).

Pollak 1987 Martha Pollak: Sullivan und die Säulenordnungen. In: Zukowsky 1987, p. 252–267.

Prestiano 1973 Robert Prestiano: The Inland Architect

– Chicago's Major Architectural Journal, 1883–1908. Ann Arbor (Michigan) (UMI) 1973.

Root 1885 John W. Root: Architectural Ornamentation. In: Inland Architect and News Record, Chicago, extra number, 1885. Quoted in: Prestiano 1973, p. 89.

Ruprich-Robert Victor-Marie-Charles Ruprich-Robert: Flore ornamentale. Paris 1866–1876.

Rykwert 1987 Joseph Rykwert: Louis Sullivan and the Gospel of Height. In: Art in America, New York, November 1987, p. 158–195.

Schuyler 1895 Montgomery Schuyler: Architecture in Chicago – Adler & Sullivan. In: Architectural Record (special series), New York, vol. 4, December 1895, p. 14–48.

Schuyler 1912 Montgomery Schuyler. The People's Savings Bank. In: Architectural Record, New York, vol. 31, no. 1, January 1912.

Semper 1860/1863 Gottfried Semper: Der Stil in den technischen und tektonischen Künsten, oder praktische Ästhetik. 2 Bände. Frankfurt am Main, München 1860, 1863.

Siry 1988 Joseph Siry: Carson Pirie Scott – Louis Sullivan and the Chicago Departement Store. Chicago, London (The University of Chicago Press) 1988.

Sprague 1979 Paul E. Sprague: The Drawings of Louis Henry Sullivan – A Catalogue of the Frank Lloyd Wright Collection at the Avery Architectural Library. Princeton (University Press) 1979.

Sullivan 1887 Louis H. Sullivan: What is the Just Subordination, in Architectural Design, of Details to Mass? In: Inland Architect & News Record, Chicago, vol. 9, no. 5, April 1887, p. 51–54 (reprinted in: Twombly 1988, p. 36–39).

Sullivan 1891 Louis H. Sullivan: The High Building Question. In: The Graphic, vol. 5, December 1891, p. 405 (reprinted in: Twombly 1988, p. 76–79).

Sullivan 1892 Louis H. Sullivan: Ornament in Architecture. In: Engineering Magazine: vol. 3, August 1892, p. 633–644 (reprinted in Twombly 1988; deutsche Übersetzung: Paul 1962, S. 130–139).

Sullivan 1896 Louis H. Sullivan: The Tall Office Building Artistically Considered. In: Lippincott's, vol. 57, March 1896, p. 403–409 (reprinted in: Twombly 1988, p. 103–113; deutsche Übersetzung in: Paul 1962, S. 144–149).

Sullivan 1901/1902 Louis H. Sullivan: Kindergarten Chats. In: Interstate Architect & Builder: February 16th 1901 – February 8th 1902 (revised 1918; first publication in bookform: 1934; quoted after the 1979 edition, New York, Dover).

Sullivan 1922/1923 Louis H. Sullivan: The Autobiography of an Idea. In: AIA Journal: June 1922 – September 1923 (first publication in bookform: 1924; reprinted 1956, New York, Dover).

Sullivan 1924 Louis H. Sullivan: A System of Architectural Ornament According with a Philosophy of Man's Power. 1924 (Facsimile mit deutscher Übersetzung in: Louis H. Sullivan. Ornament und Architektur. The Art Institute of Chicago (ed.), Tübingen 1990).

Taine 1871 Hippolyte A. Taine: History of English Literature. 2 volumes. London (Chatto & Windus) 1871.

Taine 1865/1869 Hippolyte A. Taine: La Philosophie de l'art. 1865–1869.

Twombly 1986 Robert Twombly: Louis Sullivan – His Life and Work. New York (Viking) 1986.

Twombly 1988 Robert Twombly: Louis Sullivan – The Public Papers. Chicago, London (The University of Chicago Press) 1988.

Venturi 1966 Robert Venturi: Complexity and Contradiction in Architecture. New York (Museum of Modern Art) 1966 (deutsche Übersetzung: Komplexität und Widerspruch in der Architektur. Bauwelt-Fundamente Nr. 50. Braunschweig 1978).

Vinci 1989 John Vinci: The Trading Room – Louis Sullivan and The Chicago Stock Exchange. Chicago (The Art Institute) 1989.

Weingarden 1987 Lauren S. Weingarden: Louis H. Sullivan: The Banks. Foreword by Kenneth Frampton. London, Cambridge (Mass.) (MIT Press) 1987.

de Wit 1986 Wim de Wit (ed.): Louis Sullivan – The Function of Ornament. New York, London (Norton) 1986.

Wright 1924 Frank Lloyd Wright: Louis Sullivan – His Work. In: Architectural Record, New York, vol. 56, July 1924, no. 1, p. 28–32.

Wright 1949 Frank Lloyd Wright: Genius and the Mobocracy. London (Secker & Warburg) 1949 (a chapter printed first in: Architectural Review, London, vol. 105, no. 630, June 1949, p. 295–298).

van Zanten 1986 David van Zanten: Sullivan to 1890. In: de Wit 1986, p. 13–63.

Zukowsky 1987 John Zukowsky (ed.): Chicago Architektur 1872–1922 – Die Entstehung der kosmopolitischen Architektur. München 1987 (English version: Chicago Architecture 1872–1922 – Birth of a Metropolis. Chicago, The Art Institute, 1987).

Bildnachweis

Illustration Credits

American Architect and Building News, New York: 60 (vol. 17, no. 481); 106 (vol. 50, no. 1032); 109 (vol. 50, no. 1033).

Architectural Record, New York: 82 (vol. 17, p. 487 and 478); 140 (vol. 31, p. 45); 141 oben/above, Mitte/middle (vol. 31 p. 52, 57); 145 (vol. 39, p. 460).

Art Bulletin, New York: 81 oben/above (vol. 67, no. 2, p. 289).

Art in America, New York: 118 links oben/above left (vol. 75, p. 164).

Art Institute of Chicago, Chicago, Illinois: 8; 49 unten/below; 83 oben/above; 134 oben/above.

Ausstellung neuerer amerikanischer Baukunst, Ausstellungskatalog, Berlin, Akademie der Künste, 1926: 44.

The Architecture of Frank Furness, Ausstellungskatalog, Philadelphia, Museum of Art, 1973: 13.

The Avery Library, Columbia University, New York: 21.

Bankers Magazine, New York: 141 unten/below (vol. 66).

Flynn Battaglia Architects, Buffalo, New York: 116 Mitte/middle.

Janos Bonta: Ludwig Mies van der Rohe. Berlin, 1983: 158 oben/above.

H. Allen Brooks: The Prairie School – Frank Lloyd Wright and his Midwest Contemporaries. New York, 1976: 136; 138 links/left.

Linda L. Chapman (ed.): Louis H. Sullivan – Architectural Ornament Collection. Edwardsville, Southern Illinois University, 1981: 101 rechts/right.

Chicago Historical Society, Chicago, Illinois: 50 unten/below; 52; 53; 55; 76; 96 unten/below; 97 oben/above; 111 oben rechts/above right; 121 unten/below; 122; 126.

Colorado Historical Society, Denver, Colorado; 81 unten/below.

Commission on Chicago Landmarks (Tim Samuelson): 102; 103 unten/below.

Croquis d'Architecture, Paris: 34 oben/above (vol. 2,

no. 2); 40 (vol. 3, no. 4 plate 2); 90 rechts/right (vol. 11, no. 12, plate 2).

Engineering News: 95 (13 February, 1892, Supplement).

Sigfried Giedion: Raum, Zeit, Architektur. Zürich, München 1976: 129 oben/above.

Charles E. Gregersen: Dankmar Adler. His Theatres and Auditoriums. Athens, Ohio University Press, 1990: 27; 50 oben/above; 62; 63; 65; 72 oben/above, Mitte/middle; 80; 90 links/left.

Hastings & Chivetta Architects, St. Louis, Missouri: 88 oben/above, unten rechts/below right.

Inland Architect and News Record, Chicago: 64 (vol. 5, no. 2); 84 (vol. 18, no. 4); 96 oben/above (vol. 17, no. 4); 104 oben/above (vol. 19, no. 4); 121 oben/above (vol. 36, no. 2); 134 unten/below (vol. 52, no. 4); 135 (vol. 52, no. 4).

Journal of the Society of Architectural Historians: 100 (vol. 29, p. 183); 104 unten/below (vol. 50, p. 264).

Library of Congress, Washington, D. C.: 58; 123.

Narcisco G. Menocal: Architecture as Nature – The Transcendentalist Idea of Louis Sullivan. Madison, The University of Wisconsin Press, 1981: 138 rechts/right.

Norwest Bank Minnesota South, Owatonna, Minnesota: 132 oben/above; 133 unten/below.

Robin Middleton, David J. Watkin: Architektur der Neuzeit. Stuttgart 1977: 18; 59 oben/above.

Sarah C. Mollman (ed.): Louis Sullivan in the Art Institute of Chicago. New York, London, 1989: 19 rechts/right; 57; 92 oben/above; 93 oben/above; 103 oben/above; 143 oben rechts/above right; 143 unten/below; 152.

Museum of the City of New York, New York (The Wirts Collection): 109.

Richard Nickel Committee, Chicago, Illinois: 51; 52; 56; 59 unten/below; 61; 66; 74 unten/below; 79 unten/below; 92; 93; 105; 139; 153 unten/below.

Jeffrey Karl Ochsner: H. H. Richardson – Complete Ar-

chitectural Works. London, Cambridge, MIT Press 1982: 143 oben links/above left.

David R. Phillips, Chicago, Illinois (Chicago Architectural Photographing Company): 25 Mitte/middle; 34 unten/below; 39; 67; 70/71; 72; 73; 75; 77; 78; 83 unten/below; 85; 91; 97 unten/below; 99 oben/above; 101 links/left; 107; 108; 112; 113; 115; 116 unten/below; 117 oben/above; 128; 131 unten/below; 132 unten rechts/below right; 133 oben/above; 137; 147 unten/below; 148/149; 150; 151; 154; 155; 157; 159; 160; 161; 162.

Prairie School Review, Park Forest, Illinois: 144 (vol. 10, no. 4).

Revue générale de l'architecture, Paris: 74 oben rechts/above right (vol. 11, plate 24); 29 (vol. 37, plate 30).

St. Paul's United Methodist Church, Cedar Rapids, Iowa: 142.

Joseph Siry: Carson Pirie Scott – Louis Sullivan and the Chicago Departement Store. Chicago, London, University of Chicago Press, 1988: 125; 129 unten/below.

Skidmore, Owings & Merrill, Architects, Chicago, Illinois: 98; 99 unten/below.

Paul E. Sprague: The Drawings of Louis Henry Sullivan. Princeton, University Press, 1979: 49 oben/above; 116 oben/above; 147 oben/above.

Louis H. Sullivan: A System of Architectural Ornament According with a Philosophy of Man's Power, together with Drawings for The Farmers' and Merchants' Union Bank of Columbus, Wisconsin. New York, 1967: 158 rechts/right; 163 links/left.

Louis H. Sullivan: A System of Architectural Ornament According with a Philosophy of Man's Power. Faksimile, hrsg. vom Art Institute of Chicago. Tübingen, 1990: 163 links/left.

US Postal Service: 131 oben rechts/above right.

John Vinci: The Trading Room. Chicago: The Art Institute, 1989: 74 oben links/above left; 111 oben links/above left; 112 oben/above.

Larry A. Viskochil: Chicago at the Turn of the Century in Photographs. New York, Dover, 1984: 31 unten links und rechts/below left and right; 87 oben/above.

Lauren S. Weingarden: Louis H. Sullivan; The Banks. London, Cambridge, MIT Press, 1987: 131 oben links/above left; 156.

Western Architect, Chicago: 146 (vol. 23, February 1916).

Wim de Wit (ed.): Louis Sullivan – The Function of Ornament. New York, London, 1986: 16; 19 links/left; 88 unten links/below left; 111; 117 unten/below.

Frank Lloyd Wright: Genius and the Mobocracy. London, 1949: 23.

John Zukowsky (Hrsg.): Chicago Architektur 1872–1922. München, 1987: 12; 14; 24; 25 oben/above; 25 unten/below; 31 oben/above; 87 unten/below; 88 Mitte/middle; 89; 120; 127.